The Statesman

A Study of the Role
of Charles Haughey
in the Ireland
of the future

JOHN M. FEEHAN

The morale is to the physical as three is to one
– NAPOLEON BONAPARTE

THE MERCIER PRESS
CORK and DUBLIN

The Mercier Press Limited
4 Bridge Street, Cork
24 Lower Abbey Street, Dublin 1

© John M. Feehan, 1985

Feehan, John M.
    The Statesman: A study of the role of Charles J. Haughey in the Ireland of
    the future.
    1. Haughey, Charles J.
    I. Title
    941.70824'092'4   DA965.H3

    ISBN 0 85342 761 5

Printed by Litho Press Co., Midleton, Co. Cork.

Books by the same author:
AN IRISH PUBLISHER AND HIS WORLD
TOMORROW TO BE BRAVE
THE WIND THAT ROUND THE FASTNET SWEEPS
THE MAGIC OF THE KERRY COAST
THE MAGIC OF THE SHANNON
AN IRISH BEDSIDE BOOK
THE SHOOTING OF MICHAEL COLLINS
BOBBY SANDS AND THE TRAGEDY OF NORTHERN IRELAND
OPERATION BROGUE

Contents

Introduction

I suppose you are at your old trade again: scribble, scribble, scribble.
– THE BLOODY DUKE OF CUMBERLAND to GIBBONS

This book is in the nature of a sequel to *Operation Brogue* where I described the efforts, especially of MI6, to destroy Charles Haughey and of his triumph over those attempts.

This extraordinary triumph raises a new question – where does Haughey go from here? What is his future in the days ahead in Ireland? I think it would be somewhat foolhardy to try to forecast what is going to happen. I do not know what Mr Haughey will do, so therefore I can only try to project how a real statesman might handle our desperate situation. It is unlikely Mr Haughey would agree with all my conclusions but I can only present the picture as I see it and not necessarily as Mr Haughey sees it. What is clear, however, is that, taking into account the available leadership material in Dáil Éireann, he is head and shoulders above anyone else. This seems to be universally accepted, even by British commentators.

The main theme of the book is that there are no *purely economic answers to our present disasters. There are only patriotic ones.* If we emerge as patriots we can solve them. If we continue in our present state, dominated by secularism and greed, we are doomed. This theme runs counter to the ideas now being put forward by many academics and by a large section of the media. Idealism is out of fashion, temporarily. Nations, however, are not saved by following fashionable drifts – nor are they saved by admen. Can Mr Haughey reverse the trend by giving us back our self-respect and some of our traditional ideals and in this way make the Irish people live again? I have tried to come to grips with such concepts in this book.

In the first chapter I have developed the main theme of the book in a special way but I have also dealt with something I have always found both hurtful and humiliating, namely our slave mentality. This unfortunately is a reality and not an illusion but because it is so degrading we tend to deny it. We seem to be forever grovelling, forever trying to please the British, forever on our knees begging for a nod of recognition. The whole British ethos seems to invariably get priority, especially in sections of our media as well as among many politicians. When Garret FitzGerald tells us that there is not enough money available for recommended pay increases or for the creation of jobs he is not presenting the full picture, which is that the money *is* there but the priorities are such that British interests come first. We are spending one million pounds per day protecting British interests on the Border – money which should be available for pay increases and productive economic investment. I am putting forward the suggestion that to reverse the mentality which accepts such fawning will be Haughey's first task. Idealism must always be based on hard cold realism.

In the second chapter I am really pleading that the *truth be faced*. Due to the weakness of our slave mind and to a superb propaganda exercise we have been hoodwinked right, left and centre concerning the Six Counties. The occupation of these counties is a strategic necessity for Britain and she does not care a damn about Protestants or Catholics or what they do to each other so long as she can hold on. This simple basic truth seems to have passed over the heads of much of our media and many of our politicians. Largely because of our weak perceptions here we do not seem to have the courage or the mettle to stand up to her. We lack guts, stamina and backbone. We are constantly advised to be docile towards the unionists and the British in case they make trouble and we accept that advice. Golda Meir, when Prime Minister of Israel, was fed the exact same line: 'Be nice to the Arabs – they can cause so much trouble'. Golda Meir, however, had no slave mind. She hit back by saying: 'Very well. If that is the case *we will create the trouble*', and she did. The British, the Americans and the Arabs pulled in their horns and yielded.

Regularly I come face to face with a problem – or rather a question – which few are willing to answer. It is this: *What is the basis for assuming that the British will leave the Six Counties without being forced to do so by violence?* I have asked that question of politicians, academics, writers and journalists to the point where I have become almost a bore, yet nobody will give me a straight answer. Those whom I ask cough and hum and haw and make pious noises about the evils of violence – but my question always remains unanswered – that is if one excepts Sinn Féin. There is no ambivalance in their answer.

They point out that of the thirty-odd countries which Britain occupied and left, they withdrew from *none* as a result of constitutional means only. All countries had to use violence, bloodshed and killing before Britain left. This is their track record. Violence is the only language the British understand. Apart from many international examples Sinn Féin also quote the examples of Pearse, Collins, De Valera, Lemass and scores of others who used violence and scorned constitutional means to get the British out of Ireland. Indeed De Valera, when he was Taoiseach, said that if he had an army strong enough he would invade the North.

Now I have to admit that this line of argument impresses me as being clear and logical, however regrettable; but I do wish somebody would come forward and, using the same clear logic as Sinn Féin, explain why the British are likely to respond to constitutional means when their entire history proves the opposite. Has Mrs Thatcher suddenly become a St Francis of Assisi?

I am suggesting in this book that Haughey will have to hit the British right, left and centre with everything we have got in the political domain as a beginning. De Valera did it and after a long struggle (1932-1938) he wore them down and won some major concessions. What is most noteworthy here, however, is he won election after election during the worst of the economic war. People have an instinct for recognising a great leader who is strong and decisive and who has the ability to stand up to the British.

The third chapter deals with the activities of the British Secret Service in Ireland and here I try to show that their activities are widespread in all facets of Irish life and that the Coalition seems unable or unwilling to contain them. Unless they are stopped quickly they will spread and develop like a cancerous growth and will do irreparable damage, not only to the soul of the nation, but also to its material welfare. Many do not realise that the stifling of a nation economically, to whatever point desired by the British, is part of the task of MI6. They have both the expertise and the experience to carry out such tasks effectively. Like

Nero, who fiddled while Rome burned, the Coalition are fiddling while the nation is being strangled by those people who have superbly manipulated sections of our media into unwittingly helping them.

In the fourth chapter I have singled out three diseased components in our national structure which require immediate surgery – the Civil Service, the Foreign Service and the Department of Justice. These are three grey areas that are badly decayed. Here, I suggest, there will have to be a massive restructuring, and a massive injection of new vitamins if these departments are not to drag the whole nation down still further.

In the last chapter I have looked at some of Haughey's statesmanlike qualities which are likely to help in the rebuilding of the country. All the evidence shows that he has the necessary qualities to bring this task to a successful conclusion. My only reservations lie in the area of political ruthlessness. The British and Americans, especially those who profess to care about Ireland, will trick him if they can – either by threats or flattery or both – indeed the Americans are expert in the field of flattery. For the foreseeable future it might be a good idea to say no, no, no, to every suggestion put forward, particularly by the Americans, as they are, in reality, the British back-door to Ireland. The opposite policy has been tried and failed.

Right through the book I have tried to emphasise a fundamental truth, namely, *the enemies of Ireland are the British – not the Unionists, the UDA or the IRA*. Too many Irish politicians have failed to examine thoroughly the realities of the British dimension and have preferred to take the road of self-delusion because it is the easiest, most comfortable and most financially rewarding one. Such people, however, should remember that the career of any political leader who fails to grasp the truth about the British is doomed, as indeed we know from sad experience.

In the final chapter I have also taken a look at what new dirty tricks MI6 will get up to to vilify and destroy Haughey. I have probably only touched the tip of the ice-berg here. They have hundreds of years of experience in this field to call upon and I am sure I have not uncovered even a fraction. However, it might be an interesting exercise for some of our abler journalists to keep a sharp eye open and report to the Irish people what is afoot.

At the end of October 1985 this book was ready to print. It was suggested that I should hold over publication until after the supposed 'summit' due to be held in November. I did not think it necessary to do so because I have no reason to believe that this 'summit' will be very different from others. To help the Coalition the British may make a few trivial and unimportant concessions but the harsh reality of the Six Counties will remain: brutalities, injustices, suppression, 'shoot to kill', plastic bullets, torture and murder – and the Irish taxpayer will be expected to pay even more to support this. It would be better for everyone except the British if the 'summit' did not take place.

In the foreward to *Operation Brogue* I felt constrained to write the following words:

> I would like to mention the eagerness in the past of certain critics to put words in my mouth which I never uttered. While they admitted I did not say certain things, they suggested I 'implied them'. I want to make it clear that I say what I say and I 'imply' nothing. This book does not in any way imply or suggest or insinuate that those who oppose Mr Haughey or who have written, spoken or acted against him, are disloyal to their country and are knowingly promoting the British cause in Ireland or are part of OPERATION BROGUE. They must be credited with acting according to their lights and doing the job of work given to them in the best way they see possible. These remarks, of course, apply also to critics of others in the public eye. Here and there throughout the book I may criticise people's behaviour or actions. I am, however, not criticising their worth.

All these words apply to this book with equal force.

I should like to point out that I neither interviewed Mr Haughey nor discussed this book with him. I told him before I started that I was writing it and of the general line I was taking. Other than that, the first he will see of its contents will be when it appears in the shops. Neither did I discuss the writing of any of my books with him. He did, however, once compliment me by saying that he thought *The Wind that Round the Fastnet Sweeps* was one of the best travel books he ever read. He made no comment on *Operation Brogue* – and neither did I.

I want to thank all those who helped me, particularly the very many Irish journalists who gave me the benefit of their knowledge and experience. The editors of The Mercier Press deserve my gratitude for their painstaking work on the final typescript.

Finally a word of thanks to my lawyers for their careful and thorough scrutiny of the final proofs, thus saving me from many a pitfall.

J.M.F.
October 1985

1: The Agony of Ireland

Irish army officers should not be training in a foreign country but in England or one of the dominions.
— DESMOND FITZGERALD

It is difficult to get a man to understand something when his salary depends on his not understanding it.
— UPTON SINCLAIR

We look nervously to our British masters to find out how much good we may believe of ourselves.
— D. P. MORAN

Perhaps we've lived with losing for so long that we need it like a junkie needs a fix. . . But then no one, not even Mrs Thatcher, has ever questioned our talent for defeat.
— RISTEARD Ó MUIRITHILE in *Magill* magazine

I begin this chapter by quoting some extracts from a speech and I invite my readers to guess who the speaker was. The extracts are as follows:

> The duty of Republicans to my mind is clear. They must do their part to secure common action by getting into position along the most likely line of the nation's advance. If you want to know what the direction of that line of advance at this moment is, ask yourselves what line a young man would be likely to take – a young man, let us say, with strong national feelings, honest and courageous, but without set prejudices or any commitments of his past to hamper him – who aimed solely at serving the national cause and bringing it to a successful issue.

> Such a young man would see, to begin with, the country partitioned – North separated from South. . . Were he a young man who believed that only by force would freedom ultimately be won, he would be confirmed still more in his belief in the accuracy of this analysis. He would realise that a successful uprising in arms of a subject people is made almost impossible whilst an elected national government *under contract with the enemy to maintain his overlordship* (italics mine) stands in the way, with a native army at its command. The prospective horrors of a civil war alone are

a sufficient initial deterrent to prevent any effective organisation for such an uprising. He would conclude, therefore, that the necessary condition for a successful national advance in any direction was the removal of a government subservient to the foreign master from *de facto* control here in the Twenty-six Counties. . .

The conclusions of this young man indicate, I am certain, the line the nation will take ultimately. My advice to Republicans, and to all true Irishman and women, is to take it now and save, perhaps, decades of misery and futility.

One might be forgiven for suspecting that the speaker was Gerry Adams or Martin McGuiness. In fact it was Eamon de Valera on the occasion of the founding of the Fianna Fáil party in Dublin on 16 May 1926. .

He went on to emphasise that political freedom alone was not enough. He wanted the restoration of the language, the promotion of Irish culture and above all the economic welfare of the Irish people. He concluded with the following:

Irishmen know that it is as good for them to strive to free their country from the power of the foreigner as it is for the Englishman or the Belgian or the Frenchman to free his country. Patriotism which is a virtue elsewhere cannot be a sin in Ireland; and if one section of the community arrogates to itself the right to make it so, is it to be believed that those who are thus wrongly outlawed will merely submit and will not strive day and night to free themselves from the injustice? To sit on the safety valve is a notoriously dangerous expedient.

Sixty years have passed since he delivered that address, without doubt one of the most important of his career. Fianna Fáil, the party he founded that day, went on to win election after election, to form government after government, to remain in office, with a few short breaks, for almost all of that period. One might, therefore, expect that they would, during this long span in power, have ensured that those ideals he put before them that day would be realised and that never again would 'an elected government under contract with the enemy to maintain his overlordship' sit in an Irish parliament.

What in fact is the reality, the *realpolitik* of the situation? If such a young man as he referred to were to exist today (1985) what would he see? Would he be thrilled by Ireland's progress in every sphere? Unfortunately the answer is 'No'!

The harsh reality is that he would see part of his country still occupied, and large sections of his people indifferent to the brutalities of that occupation. He would see elected Irish governments still seemingly 'under contract with the enemy to maintain his overlordship' and yielding to every British request to suppress Nationalism. He would see one million pounds of Irish people's money being spent every day to fill our jails with young Irish men and to keep soldiers of the Irish Republic and Irish police along the Border to protect British interests and ensure the occupation of part of his country by force of arms.

He would see the Irish language virutally lost and his own nation, Ireland, the only nation in the world where the native language is not an essential subject in the educational curriculum. He would discover that when Mr de Valera made that famous speech there were a quarter of a million people using the Irish language as their everyday mode of expression, while today it is used by less than twenty thousand souls.

He would see a native radio and television service unduly occupied with the presentation of a British way of life, British personalities, British sport and British royalty. On the other hand he would find the transmission of a substantial number of Irish songs discouraged in case they might encourage resistance to the British and a whole section of elected representatives representing national ideals, prevented by law from giving their views, while at the same time representatives of the occupying forces and representatives of a regime now accepted by all clear-thinking people as criminal are given the full freedom of our air waves.

It is hardly necessary for me to write of what he would find in the economic field. It is all too painfully obvious: daily bankruptcies, crippling taxation, more profitable not to work than to work, massive unemployment increasing daily, a mood of endless sick despair, a future without hope, producing teenage suicides, drugs, rape and even murder.

What might make such a young man feel extremely bitter would be the obscene, sickening practice of 'jobs for the boys' which is so glaring under the present Coalition government and which so effectively belies the idealistic and altruistic election promises upon which the government was sold. We were to have

a new Ireland, a new integrity in Irish politics, a new crusade
of honesty and reputability. Charles Haughey was the shifty one.
Garret was the man of integrity and uprightousness. But what
actually happened? Scarcely a week passes when some Coalition
supporter is not given a plum job at a high salary and most of
them seem to have no special qualifications for the jobs other
than they have been Fine Gael or Labour election workers.
What is even more ironic is that the Irish people, who were to
be freed from this disgraceful patronage, now have to put their
hand in their pockets and pay these salaries, perks and pensions.
Our hypothetical young man might feel justly angered and might
well drastically revise his ideas as to who are the dishonest and
shifty ones.

This is but a miniature picture of what such a young man
would find in Ireland in the 1980s. Perhaps what might puzzle
him most of all would be the realisation that not only were the
idealistic utterances of Garret FitzGerald put to one side, but
the Fianna Fáil party itself contributed substantially, particularly
during the 1970s, to this disastrous state of affairs. This is the
Ireland which came out of Mr De Valera's speech at the founding
of Fianna Fáil on that far off day in May 1926 when he held out
the vision of the promised land to the Irish people.

What went wrong? When did the rot set in? If we want to
avoid a revolution how can we remedy it and prevent it happen-
ing again? Does the hope of achieving this rest in the hands of
one man?

There are several factors involved in this catastrophe, most
of them adequately dealt with in Kevin Boland's two books: *The
Rise and Decline of Fianna Fáil* and *Fine Gael: British or Irish?*.
Here, however, I will concentrate on two elements very closely
interlinked ‒ elements which have largely been overlooked by
commentators and writers: (1) the pathetic slave mind of large
sections of the Irish people and (2) the steady desertion of
national ideals due to superb British propaganda.

The inter-twining of these two elements has played a crucial
role in bringing Ireland to its present state of destitution. Our
economic disasters are only symptoms which have their roots in
one or both of them.

The first element is best portrayed by a short parable. Supposing a farmer planted a number of sally-tree saplings in a field,

bent each one over and tied the top to the ground so that they made a U-loop. If then, after say twenty years when the trees were fully grown, he cut the rope binding them to the ground they would not all immediately spring upwards. The straightening out would be a very slow process. After a period of years some few would be standing upright; others would be half bent and still others would have remained quite close to the ground.

In many ways there is an analogy between those sally trees and the Irish people. For hundreds of years we were, so to speak, tied to the ground, trampled into pulp, treated like animals, crushed and tortured as badly as the negro slaves. Then suddenly we got our freedom and unfortunately many were unable to take it. Like the prisoners of the Bastille, coming from darkness to light, who resented being disturbed, it was too much for them. They had come to love their degrading servitude and they remained on their knees, still grovelling before their masters, still wearing the invisible chains of slavery. Sixty years later they have advanced from their knees to a half-crouch position but are still bent over. It will probably take another few generations before they can bring themselves to stand erect and raise their heads in pride and dignity.

It would be wrong to suggest that a majority of Irish people fit that description. Indeed this is far from being so. Nevertheless even a superficial investigation would show that a fair proportion of our population, largely concentrated in the cities and in positions of responsibility, are still on their knees hoping their betters will honour them with a lash.

In the past these people have been referred to as the Dublin 4 set, probably because RTÉ is situated in that area. They have always been with us under different names, West Britons, Half-Sirs, etc. They are now generally referred to as the new Irish Yuppies. Yuppieism is a kind of sub-culture which acknowledges in a most servile way the superiority of foreign trappings over a native culture. Their great catch-cry is 'pluralism'. They do not really know what it means. They think it means the removal of any religious influence in public affairs. That is exactly what it does *not* mean, as any good dictionary could tell them, but it sounds important and to be associated with what is important as distinct from what is *real* is vital sustenance to them.

For them the capital of Ireland is London and they pay extraordinary homage to any person with the blue blood, however stupid or dense that person may be. Most of their ideas, when they have any, are taken from England and their lives are heavily influenced by formulae driven into their heads by the incursions of British television and British newspapers. These attitudes seem to have produced such a deep lack of confidence in themselves that they must perforce turn to England for moral support, since they are always pretending to be something they are not. They can be regularly seen travelling in first-class compartments reading the up-market British newspapers and at the same time making sure that the other occupants of the carriage see what they read. They are little more than adult babies still in mental diapers. 'They buy books they don't understand,' says D.P. Moran. 'They go to plays they don't appreciate; they pay their shillings to enter into a picture gallery out of which they take nothing but a headache.'

In a much more telling passage the same writer describes them as they were in his day:

> The concrete absurdities which our position as tail to England throws us into are infinite. They are before our eyes at every turn. When an English actor of eminence visits us don't we cheer ourselves hoarse and the next day when he says something gracious about us in the columns of the evening papers we beam all over our faces and add an inch to our stature. We call it hospitality, warm Irish welcome, anything but what it is, self-debasement, servility and cringe. The shifts and twists and turns of the respectable Irish to behave after their absurd second-hand conceptions of English ladies and gentlemen – the antics they play, the airs they assume are full of the comic element, but the sad slavishness of it all is what strikes the Irish observer. The most disagreeable thing about all this cringe is its needlessness and absolutely false basis. The appeal to Irish history condemns it. It is sad to see an unfortunate wretch whining under the lash of whip; it is, however, natural to whine under such circumstances. But it is revolting to see people whining for no adequate reason whatever.

Many of these yuppies flocked to the standard of the new Fine Gael and some obtained positions of influence within that organisation. Attracted by the pro-British direction it was taking they could feel quite at home as part of that group and they were by no means unmindful of the financial rewards that might come their way if they behaved in the proper spirit of pluralism.

Perhaps the most important section of the community who absorbed much of the yuppie philosophy to the terrible detriment of the nation is the Irish civil service.

In 1922, when Dublin Castle was taken over by the fledgling Irish government, they effectively took over the building and the furniture only. The vast majority of the personnel remained British in outlook and British in loyalties. C. S. Andrews in his book *Man of No Property* says:

> The Irish civil service had been set up by a group of Irish and a few English officials who held fairly senior posts in the British civil service prior to the Treaty. They modelled the new bureaucracy exactly on the British administrative structure with the addition of a simulacrum of a foreign office which they called the Department of External Affairs. The organisation they created was of a form well suited to administering an empire on which the sun never sets. . .

While these civil servants carried out the functions of government with reasonable impartiality and integrity they nevertheless saw themselves primarily as colonial administrators whose lodestar was Westminster while Dublin was only one of many minor satellites. Within the organisation itself they created viewpoint-moulds, in much the same way as Lever, Lover and Edgeworth created stage-Irish moulds in literature. The end-product of these moulds was that the British were our masters, they knew best what was good for us and we could rely on their judgment. When framing new legislation most departments looked to Britain for guidelines and indeed at times slavishly copied British Acts.

Even after sixty years this subservience seems to be so deeply ingrained that we hardly ever look to countries more analogous to Ireland for legislative inspiration, countries such as Holland, Denmark, Norway, Sweden or Belgium. It has long been known that this deep-rooted inferiority expresses itself very strongly when our officials go to London for discussions. Some of them seem to melt to nothingness in the presence of a titled gent. Here they seem to get tongue-tied and lock-jawed in the presence of the arrogant British who eventually win whatever concessions they want and send the Paddies home with a patronising pat on the back. John Leyden, one time Secretary of the Department of Industry and Commerce and one of the ablest of civil servants, learnt a bitter lesson when, after years of co-operation with the British, he found when the chips were down, they treated him with utter contempt and made clear that in their view he was an inferior human being because he was Irish. Unfortunately many of our civil servants today do not seem to have learned from such experiences.

While sixty years of self-government has rid large sections of the people of their traditional servitude there are still segments in deep bondage. 'You have the phenomenon in this country that some of our civil servants and army officers are more English than the English themselves,' said Lieut-General M. J. Costello in an *Irish Times* interview with Seán Cronin. 'Their view of NATO is the view from London. . . Since the foundation of the State the Irish bureaucracy has believed that whatever was British was best. . . the Irish civil service is built on the British system. They ape and adapt British ideas.'

When you add all this together – our slave mind, our embarrassment at Irish names and symbols, our derision of the Irish language, our anglicisation of public institutions such as RTÉ, gardaí and army it becomes easier to understand why so many European statesmen hold us almost in contempt and why British politicians, such as Thatcher, feel they can kick us around as much as they like.

This, of course, brings up the interesting question as to why it should be so – why such an important section of our population should be still cowering before their so-called betters? It has, of course, a historical reason, known to all and best illustrated by the parable of the sally tree – but I have always believed there was another reason which was psychological, and since I was not competent to delve into the inner workings of the human mind I discussed the matter at length with a distinguished psychologist. This is what he explained to me:

We are all the product, not only of our parents and grandparents, but also of our great-grandparents, our great-great-grandparents and so on back for hundreds of years. Deeply embedded in everyone's psyche are what psychologists call 'race-memories', handed down through the genes from generation to generation, which through the subconscious have a profound influence on our every day actions generations later. It is more than likely that the ancestors of some of today's yuppies had, as children or babies, some deeply traumatic experience such as having to watch their families evicted on the roadside to die of cold and hunger, or witness parents dying the most appalling deaths of starvation during the Famine, or seeing one's father being forced to crawl on his knees through a long hall to hand over his rent, such as happened on the Lansdowne estate, and at the same time being kept in the kneeling position by lashes of a whip, or experiencing the agonising sight of a father or brother tied by a length of rope to the rear of a Black-and-Tan lorry and dragged along the ground while the occupants amused themselves taking pot shots and ultimately riddling the body with bullets. A little child experiencing any one of these daily occurrences would have such memories so deeply embedded in the psyche that they would surface hundreds of years later.

Such race memories, according to my psychologist friend, could have two effects. In the case of the strong-minded it could raise feelings of hostility against the rulers and this hostility could express itself in opposition and indeed even in rebellion generations later. In the case of weaker minds it could have the opposite effect: that of producing a deep sense of insecurity resulting in an exaggerated respect for his masters and inducing him to ally himself with them, do their bidding however slavish, however nauseating, in the hope that he may feel within himself some echoes of their prestige and power.

It does not seem unreasonable that this opinion has a solid basis in fact. There is plenty of evidence all around us in the Ireland of today: the strong-minded who have scorned the British influence and weak-minded 'yuppies' who are unable to lift themselves off their knees. It is surely true to say that the slavery of the past is only partly destroyed.

Most of this would be little more than amusing were it not for the fact that quite a sizeable section of this sub-culture achieved positions of influence somewhat beyond their intellectual capabilities, in government, in the civil service, in higher education and particularly in the media, and their activities have had, in some cases, calamitous effects.

This will be one of the first great tests of Charles Haughey's leadership. Can he destroy this sub-culture and replace it with something which will not only inspire a sense of national pride and dignity, but also work in a competent and intelligent way towards making the whole country a real nation. In his book *The National Ideal* Joseph Hanly wrote:

> Ireland is today at the parting of the ways. She will either go down, with her entire traditional nationality a gaunt and fading mockery, to the grave, or she will rise in glory in those same traditions, to a future greater than her past.

Those words were written fifty years ago. Sadly Ireland has gone past the parting of the ways. She is today a 'gaunt and fading mockery' but she is not yet in the grave, although the diggers are ready and the Brussels undertakers are donning their black hats. Can Haughey save her? Can he bring her back to the parting of the ways and put her on the right road?

Most of the people know what the leaders of Fine Gael think of Nationalism and Republicanism. For them Pádraig Pearse, the father of modern Irish revolutionary Nationalism is an acute embarrassment whom they would prefer to forget, despite the fact that they owe their massive salaries, perks and pensions to him and his companions who rejected constitutional politics in favour of violence. What a contrast to that ostrich attitude is Haughey's view of Pearse. Speaking at a commemoration dinner he said:

> Pearse was above all else a democrat. He believed in the sovereign people. . . to him the Republic was the people's will and the central part of Republicanism was that the people of Ireland could express their will freely.
>
> Pearse's enemies claim that the Rising of 1916 denies him the right to be called a democrat. He is reviled as a militarist, a man who glorified in war. The truth however is that Pearse sought freedom by force of arms only because there was no other way open to him in the circumstances of his time.
>
> The Defenders of the Realm were not open to political persuasion and, in any event, the Irish parliamentary party had so degraded the political process that no man or woman of sensibility or idealism could have any part of it. . .
>
> Pearse foresaw his beloved Ireland as a land in which a cultural dimension would be an essential part of everybody's every day

life. . .

Because for him the people were the nation, Pearse would if he were here today insist that all the policies and programmes of government should be directed to the welfare of the people. . .

He would seek to create a caring society where the ideal of the brotherhood of man would be translated into practical voluntary community work. . .

Pearse loved his people and sought their happiness. Although he offered them nobility and idealism his political philosophy was liberal, tolerant and progressive. . .

He believed that Ireland's history, the common past which all her men and women share, make her spiritually, emotionally, intellectually and politically one indissoluble nation. . .

The history of the people of every part of this island is one of unfulfilled aspirations, exploitation, disappointments and setbacks. We share that heritage in common. Pearse wanted a nation in which that long and troubled story could be pulled together in the achievement of greatness.

This is Haughey speaking as an Irishman who fully accepts the ideals of Pearse. There is no ambivalence, no blubbering about European defence, no 'begging your pardon, your honour', no deference to the Duke of Norfolk or the Bilderberg conference. It is a clear and inspiring statement of full commitment to the ideals of 1916.

But can he bring Ireland back to those ideals?

It seems to me there are two courses open to him: that of the small-time politician which will ensure failure and that of the statesman which will ensure success. The small-time politician will be governed absolutely by the power of the vote. The criteria by which he will make decisions will be the number of votes that can be acquired as a result of any political action, piece of legislation or speech. This will lead him into taking short term decisions, useful for the next election, but disastrous in the long term interests of the country. Not entirely absent from such a politician's mind will, of course, be the knowledge that when the chickens come home to roost he will no longer be around. If not gone to his punishment in the next world he will certainly be enjoying his massive pension and perks in this one. While making suitable noises on St Patrick's Day and Easter Week and opening the occasional Irish cultural function, he will *de facto* accept British domination over this country but, of course, he will not say so publicly. He will take no steps whatever to stir up the embers of Irish Nationalism now so skilfully smothered by British propaganda. Above all he will make absolutely sure that no effective action whatever is taken to strengthen the Irish language other than such ineffective sounds as will ensure the Gaelic vote. He will let the morale of the Irish people slip to a degree that they can no longer distinguish themselves from the people of a British shire. The consequences of this lack of national morale can only further depress the economy and might very well in the end lead to a terrible civil war.

But that is the mind of the politician and how it works. Unfortunately it has been the type of mind which dominated Irish thinking for more than a decade and *we* are now paying the price. I emphasise the word *we*, because it is not the politicians who have to put their hands in their pockets and lower their standards of living to pay. They have looked after themselves well. It is you and I and every ordinary citizen of the State who have to pay for their blunders.

It has often been said that the politician looks to the next election while the statesman looks to the next generation. I suggest that statement is only partly true. It would be more accurate to say that the good statesman looks primarily to the next generation while at the same time keeping a sharp weather eye on the next election. No matter how many of the qualities of a great statesman an individual has, these are of little use unless he is in power and to get power one must win elections and to win elections one must win votes and to win votes one must *capture the imagination of the public.*

I emphasise the words *capture the imagination of the public* strongly because it is that element in politics which wins most votes, and not always satisfaction or dissatisfaction with performance. The most memorable events in the history of all countries prove that point. People are moved by the emotions great leaders can arouse in them. When Napoleon took over the mutinous, hungry, undisciplined French army he did not offer them a constitutional crusade or a vague plan for economic recovery drawn up by some civil servant. Instead he addressed them thus:

Soldiers, you are half starved and naked. The government owes you much but can do nothing for you. Your patience, your courage, do you honour but give you no glory, no advantage. I will lead you into the most fertile plains of the world. . . there you will reap honour, glory and wealth. Soldiers, will you be wanting in courage and firmness?

In his 'blood, sweat and tears' speech Churchill did much the same for the British people. Similarly De Gaulle in France, Adenauer in Germany and Gasperi in Italy roused their peoples from the depths of despair, as did Eamon de Valera when he came to power in 1932. Who now remembers the small-time political jelly-fish who opposed them? It was this uplifting of spirit, and raising of morale that kept the great leaders in power so long and that won the votes of the people. In knowing the art of winning the imagination of the public they, at the same time, knew the art of governing them. The great statesman governs the people. The politician lets the pressure groups govern him. We get a hint of this greatness in Haughey's closing remarks at the Fianna Fáil Ard Fheis in 1984:

Fianna Fáil offers the people of Ireland an alternative to the present state of hopelessness. Our political forebears aroused the spirit of this nation before, to overcome greater difficulties and to lead the Irish people out of more daunting situations. We are not going to be the generation of Fianna Fáil who surrendered *to the defeatest neo-colonial mentality* (italics mine). Fianna Fáil will once again lead the Irish people out of the shadows of depression in a great national advance out into the sunlight of national pride and self-esteem, progress and achievement.

When Napoleon revealed his famous maxim that the 'morale is to the physical as three is to one' what he was saying was that if the morale of his troops was high he could defeat an enemy whose numerical strength was three times greater than his. If we relate that principle to the affairs of an economically broken Ireland we can conclude that if our national morale is raised to its highest point we have a three times better chance of resolving these economic difficulties. The old adage that 'trade follows the flag' is only another way of saying that trade follows a high morale. Conversely, of course, it can be said that if national morale is low, prosperity suffers heavily. The prosperity of Ireland has reached an all time low. It is surely not a coincidence that our national morale is also at an all time low.

The first of Haughey's major tasks will, therefore, be to resurrect our national morale and bring it back to life; note that I have *not* said economic conditions. These will follow as sure as night follows day. But what is national morale? How does one recognise it? There are scores of definitions in many books but they all come to the same thing. National morale is nothing more than the ageless, timeless concept we call Nationalism.

To illustrate this let us ask a few questions. How would one define a British Nationalist? I suggest that a British Nationalist is one who is proud to be British, who takes pride in his language, in his culture, in his national institutions, in the glories of his race and not least in his royal family. The same definition could be given to a German, French, Dutch or Danish Nationalist.

Now let us ask the question: What is an Irish Nationalist? One would presume that an Irish Nationalist is one who loves his country, his language, his culture and his national institutions. But that is not the case. A different standard holds for the Irish Nationalist. British propaganda has skilfully provided that standard for us. An Irish Nationalist is a terrorist who kills British soldiers and makes war on Britain and who stubbornly refuses to accept British domination over his country. We in Ireland have come to accept this definition. It has been drummed into us so often even by our own political leaders, by our media, to such an extent that we are ashamed of our language, our culture, our right to be free and our right to rid our country of its army of occupation. Such aspirations are all wrong, offensive and nasty in an Irishman but perfectly good and noble in the British, the Germans or the French. One can only be lost in admiration at the brilliance of British propaganda in making us believe this and marvel at their genius in getting Irishmen to do it for them. At the same time one cannot but despise the grovelling yuppies who not only swallowed this hook, line and sinker but who helped to promulgate it.

Joseph Hanly in his book *The National Ideal* makes the best attempt I know at describing nationality:

> This subtle influence called nationality, this force which we can feel intensely, or completely lose, and which we cannot easily define, is, all in one, the greatest educator, the greatest economic

organiser, the greatest civic guardian, and the greatest national protector that any country can have. It is, in consonance with religion, the most inspiring factor for national, social and economic greatness, and the strongest weapon against internal disunion, greed or laziness, that the combined intellect can call to its aid. . .

Countries that maintain a strong position in the economic world do so, not *in ratio to their territory, population or wealth, but in accordance with the strength of their nationality* (italics mine).

Countries that attempt to conquer or to hold other countries in subjection attack the nationality of their vicitms as a first advance, and, if possible, destroy it to gain a final hold.

The truth of this last sentence particularly must be clear to every Irishman with even a fragmentary knowledge of the history of his country. The destruction of our language, our customs, our literature, our heritage has constituted a major thrust in the destruction and occupation of our country as a whole. Today it goes on relentlessly without pause, without let-up.

I, therefore, think it is not an exaggeration to suggest that, like France in 1871, Italy in 1921, Germany and Japan in 1945, a return to a high national morale, as it was in 1921 and 1932, is the surest first step to national economic recovery.

One may reasonably argue that with our frightening unemployment, our daily bankruptcies and our ever worsening economic position, this is an area we should tackle first. I disagree. World history and particularly world economic history has shown the opposite to be the case. *Tackle the morale of the nation and all else will follow.* We know from our own history of the 1960s and 1970s that high employment and economic prosperity do not bring about a strong morale, which alone ensures permanence and continuity. It is because we lost our national identity and our national morale during those 'mohair' decades that we are where we are today.

Let me suggest an example or two of what I mean. I understand that recently officials of the Department of Social Welfare went around to secondary schools lecturing final year students on their 'dole' entitlements. This resulted in the taxpayer having to provide an extra £35,000,000 per annum to pay this 'dole'.

Supposing we had an enlightened government, who themselves had a national morale, 'and instead, sent around officials to lecture on the vital connection between 'Buy Irish' and employment, on how every piece of Irish material purchased meant more job prospects for themselves; on how to organise and protest in supermarkets where preference was given to foreign goods; on how to establish small 'Buy Irish' committees in every town who would persuade, induce and if necessary over-awe supermarkets to stock these goods. It is hardly necessary to imagine the electrifying effect this would have all over the country.

Supposing our civil servants and our trade unionists, to take numerically important categories, loved their country and their people to the extent of doing something about it instead of talk-ing and complaining – suppose the wives of these people refused to buy imported goods even if they had to do without them; refused to patronise supermarkets which did not stock at least 60% Irish goods, then one can be sure that within a short time the unemployment problem would be well on the way to a sol-ution.

It is this kind of patriotism which rebuilt Germany and Japan. It is this kind of national morale, and not gimmicky economic accountancy, that can rebuild Ireland.

It is this kind of national morale that Haughey will have to inspire in the Irish people.

Our leaders today have, unfortunately, lost their self-respect. Their constant toadying to their 'betters' limits their concept of what it is to be Irish. If ever they do learn to respect themselves as Irish they might win the right of the respect of others. That right they do not enjoy today.

How will Charles Haughey face this essential first task? To this question I cannot give an answer because it is something which is very personal and which only he himself can decide. I am not a practised, experienced politican. I do not know a great deal about the day-to-day working of the political world. I must, therefore, confine myself to a broad general principle.

The whole future of Ireland may well depend on which of two possible approaches are taken. There will be the politician's approach which will say: 'To hell with the welfare of the Irish people. We will be dead and gone by then. Let's concentrate on staying in power and getting jobs for the boys, watching our pensions and yielding to any pressure for temporary advantage.' The statesman will say: 'The Irish people have trusted me with their future. Through the ignorance, incompetence and toadyism of politicians their ideals and aspirations have been smothered by a yuppie sub-culture. The highest aim held out to them by their government has been to live as second rate citizens satisfying the whims of an alien power. I am going to put a stop to all that. It will be a long slow process but I believe when they are given back their dignity and self-respect they will support me in election after election as they did when De Valera gave them back their national pride in 1932.'

Which of these two approaches will be Haughey's? That is a question which only time can answer, but this can be said – all his recent statements and actions indicate that he is in the great national tradition of Pearse, Collins and De Valera and that his approach will be the statesman's. It would be foolish to minimise the enormity of what lies ahead of him. It is too late now to repair a broken Ireland. He must remake her from the ground up.

There is no reason to suppose that he will not respond successfully to that challenge, but it is in the first instance a challenge to idealism and patriotism. There is no reason to assume that the young Haughey who climbed the ramparts of Trinity College on VE day in 1945 to tear down the Union Jack will not now, as a more experienced and mature Haughey, remove the trappings of what that flag stands for in the life of the nation.

2: A New England Called Ireland

Britain has one of the most violent and uncivilised histories of any European country. Yet the orthodox view is that the English are both non-violent and civilised and it is the people whom Britain has oppressed who are violent and uncivilised.

— LIZ CURTIS in *The Roots of Irish Racism*

Do not have the idea that in one year, or two years, or five years, or ten years, you are going to have your country free, for if the iron of the Truce has entered your souls after six months of it and you are not prepared to fight, you will not do so after one year, two years or ten years when you have Colonial or Free State fat in your bodies.

— SEÁN ETCHINGHAM (Treaty Debate)

The British government has oppressed and degraded our people, set them at each others throats, offered the Protestants small gifts and the Catholics kicks but by doing these things controlled them both. It has brought the Protestants into disgrace and forced many good citizens to come to the conclusion that only by the gun can they bring sense into their kind of politics.

— DES WILSON in *An End to Silence*

With compatriots like these (the Irish) wouldn't you rather admit to being a pig than being Irish.

— SIR JOHN JUNOR in the *Sunday Express*

The Irish are pigs.

— HER ROYAL HIGHNESS, PRINCESS MARGARET

How can the elite of usurpers, aware of their mediocrity, establish their privileges? By one means only: debasing the colonised to exhalt themselves, denying the title of humanity to the native and defining them simply as absence of qualities — animals not humans.

— JEAN-PAUL SARTRE

Would our fathers ever have thought they would see the day when an Irish Taoiseach thumbed a lift in a British army bomber?

— RAY MacSHARRY TD

If national morale is the key to Irish recovery perhaps we should look at one tremendous obstacle which stands in the way and which has stood in the way for generations. That obstacle is the British dimension in Ireland – an obstacle which must eventually be removed if we are to make even the slightest progress towards peace. The removal of this factor is also fundamental to any economic or political advancement. This simple basic principle seems to have eluded most of our politicians and indeed a lot of our media. The skilful propaganda exercise to persuade them that the opposite is true is a credit to the brilliance of British propaganda in Ireland.

The British dimension in Ireland is twofold:

1. A forcible occupation of Six of our Thirty-Two Counties against the wishes of the vast majority of the people of this island.
2. A constant campaign, mainly directed by MI6, to depress us economically and by infiltration of our institutions of state to stifle and paralyse any expression of our national identity which does not meet with British approval.

A special chapter will be devoted to this second element.

Haughey's task of resurrecting, and indeed saving, the Irish people is intimately bound up with both elements which are now known by the more respectable name of 'Anglo-Irish relations', but is in reality nothing other then Britain's desire to occupy part of our country and hold the rest of it as a small satellite state, obedient and co-operative. He seems to have a much clearer grasp than most people of the realities here if we are to judge from a recent statement he made in the Dáil when he rightly castigated FitzGerald for his failure to grasp this principle:

> Will you never learn? Will you never understand that no matter what soft words or protestations are used the age-old reality prevails? Britain relentlessly and remorselessly pursues British self-interest no matter whom it hurts or effects.

In examining the first element of the British dimension it is important that we be brutally truthful and face the harshest facts, however unpleasant. Unfortunately we too often delude ourselves and blind ourselves to the truth. Due to superb British propaganda it is now socially acceptable to criticise the Nazis for exterminating 6,000,000 Jews, yet one is not supposed to even mention the fact that the British exterminated more than 30,000,000 in the countries they occupied. In the matter of brutality, genoicide and murder, world history proves beyond doubt that their documented record, over a longer period of time, is infinitely worse than that of Hitler and the Nazis. This is hard, cold bitter fact and when we talk of 'good Anglo-Irish relations' we must realise that these are the people with whom we must have good relations. Liz Curtis in her excellent book *The Roots of Anti-Irish Racism* puts this in perspective:

> A gigantic exercise in self-delusion has helped to preserve English pride and self-regard down the centuries. Actions taken for reasons of political and economic expedience have been presented as if altruism were the sole motive. Atrocities of all kinds – from Cromwell's massacre at Drogheda, to the slave trade, to the appropriation of vast tracts of other people's countries – have been justified by claims of religious, cultural and racial superiority. As a result many English people are unable to see themselves as others see them; to recognise why in other parts of the world the Union Jack has been described as the 'Butcher's Apron'; and the empire as 'the place where the sun never sets and the blood never dries'. . .
>
> Today these myths help them to maintain their unjust occupation of part of Ireland, to use plain English people as scapegoats for the failures of the system and to amass great wealth at the expense of the people of the Third World.

These are the British ruling classes we are dealing with; undemocratic, barbaric and uncivilised, coated over with a veneer of respectability, expressed in diplomatic, almost religious language which has deluded and fooled so many Irish politicians. Not so, of course, the ordinary decent British citizen who is also being used and exploited by this ruling class.

In order that we may get some appreciation of the nature of the task facing Haughey let us look at some of the myths which the British have so successfully palmed off on the Irish and indeed the world.

Myth No. 1. The British will leave the Six Counties when a majority there want it.

This is a complete falsehood. Britain will *not* leave the Six

Counties even if everyone there wanted her to – and there is plenty of documentary evidence to prove that. Let us ask ourselves the question: What does Britain really want in Ireland? Why has she spent billions of pounds and sacrificed so many lives trying to break us? Only a fool would believe it was for our good even though some yuppy historians might promulgate that view.

The harsh reality is that Britain believes it to be an *absolute military necessity to have a weak, disunited, divided Ireland on her western flank,* so as to rid herself of the danger of any threat from the Atlantic approaches, as well as the danger of a hostile Irish state, like Cuba and the United States. This has been her policy for hundreds of years and it is more than ever her policy today. In my book *Operation Brogue* I dealt at length with this important point and backed it up with confirming quotations from British sources. We simply have to face this harsh reality: *Britain will not leave the Six Counties unless forced to do so,* but she will continue to plug the 'altruism' line so long as she can get people to believe her. This 'altrusim' falsehood has been promulgated with great success by the British not only in Ireland and Britain, but all over the world.

The *Sunday Times,* for example, said: 'Since 1969 the main note of British policy in the Six Counties has been altruism' and again 'The notorious problem is how a civilised country can overpower uncivilised people without becoming less civilised in the process' – this at a time when the RUC were using the most excruciating torture to beat false confessions out of innocent people.

Another extraordinary example of this pompous arrogant outlook can be found in what one British journalist, Peregrine Worsthorne, wrote in the *Sunday Telegraph* as Bobby Sands lay dying:

> The English have every reason to feel proud of their country's recent record in Northern Ireland, since it set the whole world a uniquely impressive example of altruistic service in the cause of peace. Nothing done by any other country in modern times so richly deserves the Nobel prize.

Somebody should have reminded this journalist of the strong moves in the late 1930s to award the Nobel Peace prize to Hitler!

This line of civilised 'altruism' – usually in association with Christ and the twelve apostles – has been plugged in all countries of the world. But perhaps from the Irish point of view what is saddest of all is that many Irish embassies abroad, who should be opposing that line and promoting the truth, are actually supporting it. It seems as if they must first get approval from British ambassadors before they can open their mouths.

What in fact is the reality of British activity in Ireland? What is the truth we should be proclaiming to the world? For any Irishman the answers to these questions should not necessitate very much thinking or research. He would know that, not only in Ireland but, in every country in which Britain was involved she has left behind her a trail of slaughter, murder, pillage and terror. But unlike the Nazis, who were brutally honest about what they were doing, Britain tried to cover up her butchery under the cloak of altruism and benevolence. When we look dispassionately at her track record we will hardly find a single colony which she left without blood-stained hands. Here in Ireland no one needs to be reminded of the millions she liquidated. I imagine there is hardly an Irish person who reads this book who has not had an ancestor in the not-too-distant past either jailed, tortured, murdered or sold into slavery by the British. Alone among the democracies of the free world, she shares with the Nazis the distinction of having been condemned by an International Court of Justice for torture and inhuman conduct. Even today she is continuing this in the Six Counties, but in a more camouflaged way: torture, murder of innocent people, brutality, corrupt courts etc. The list is endless. Speaking in Dáil Éireann Charles Haughey said:

> Some mornings ago I found myself listening to the radio and hearing the man who was responsible for recruiting mercenaries for Angola state clearly and positively that it was recognised today that British soldiers who have served in the North were the most desirable and best type of mercenary for this work. That man made the positive and definite statement. It is difficult for us not to be emotional when we hear that sort of thing and then realise that is the sort of situation that exists in the six north-eastern counties of this land of ours.

We have now become used to British politicians pouring forth worthless speeches of impenetrable verbiage about reconciling the traditions of Northern Ireland when most of them know quite well that Britain does not want to bring the traditions together and that their high-sounding speeches are nothing more than massive red herrings designed to camouflage the fact that she wants to occupy the Six Counties for strategic purposes, and that, irrespective of the interests or wishes of the people living there, or how many are killed, she will continue to do so.

Writing in 1984 Desmond Fennell had this to say:

> It is important to remind ourselves that British propaganda in Ireland and throughout the world has had, and has, one chief aim with regard to the North, namely to smother and discourage anger about the injustice being done there, and to excite anger solely and exclusively against the rebellion which that injustice has provoked. And it is primarily because this propaganda has been so successful, particularly in the Republic, that the horror of the North has continued for fifteen years and shows no sign of ending.

Britain will leave only when it is militarily advantageous to her or when she is forced out. This is the harsh reality which has to be faced and dealt with if Ireland is to survive as a free nation. So far, few of our oratorical constitutional politicians have faced up to it.

Myth No. 2. In Ireland there are two nations

It is important for Britain to promulgate this falsehood because in doing so it strengthens her claim that the Six Counties are part of Britain, and Ireland has no claim to them. There are, of course, *not* two nations. There is one nation only with different traditions. They say, with tongue in cheek, that because the Northern Unionists want to remain with Britain, therefore, it is a separate nation. What is *not* said is that a majority in pockets of Wales and Scotland do not want to remain with Britain. Why are they not allowed to cede? I imagine a majority of the Dublin 4 set would like to be British. Have they the right to cede? If the principle of majority rule in pockets of a country were accepted then the southern part of the United States would now be an independent nation. Lincoln fought a bitter war on that issue.

The British know quite well that there is only one nation with a privileged group in occupation of one part of it – and they support that group for their own interests. There are, of course, two traditions in the North and to this one can only say 'so what?' There are three traditions in the Republic – the Gaelic, the Irish and the Anglo-Irish. In Switzerland, Belgium, France, the United States and other countries there are many different traditions. The existence of different traditions in a country does not mean that each tradition must have its own political independence. The Bavarian Catholics can co-exist side by side with Prussian Protestants. Ethnic differences of peoples in Yugoslavia, Italy, France and the Soviet Union do not prevent them working together. In all these countries the various traditions are able to live and work in harmony but the desire of one tradition to be overlord and to have all the goodies is the reason why the two traditions in the Six Counties cannot work together. The politically unrealistic outlook of some Southern Irish politicians that we must make fundamental changes in our Constitution to satisfy one tradition is an example of the poor grasp these politicians have of the whole Northern question. They do not seem to understand that if we turned our Constitution upside down and inside out it would not make the slightest difference. The Unionists want to hold on to the privileges given them by the British, particularly jobs, housing, industry, their total domination of all aspects of life, and they have already treated with utter contempt any suggestion of changes in our Constitution.

There is now a possibility that the Nationalists may soon outnumber them but Harold McCusker, Unionist MP, recently made it clear that even in such an event they would not accept a United Ireland. Majority rule for Unionists only operates when it suits themselves. The Unionists struggle in the Six Counties is about 'goodies' and not about 'gods'.

It is important, of course, to point out that the Unionists, in the eyes of the British, are just more Irish scum, but they support them and give them privileges because they can rely on them to do their bidding and hold the Six Counties for them. The greatest fear of the British is that the Unionists and Nationalists might come together and that they will try to prevent at all costs.

One of the favourite propaganda lines put into circulation by the British is that if they leave the Six Counties there will be a Unionist backlash, a blood bath, a civil war. *There is no evidence whatever to support this theory.* The track record of the Unionists is that for seventy years they have been ranting and shouting about spilling blood and fighting all and sundry but the hard reality is that they have very prudently kept well away from the fighting line. The IRA, who made no blood-curdling speeches, were the people who fought a long and bitter war from 1916 to 1921. The Unionists, despite their speeches, confined themselves to beating drums, waving banners and hiding safely behind the protection of the British army. One Unionist paramilitary leader put it succinctly: 'Do you think we are going to fight and die to put Paisley, Molyneaux and Smyth in power. Not bloody likely.'

With the protection of the British army gone the tough, hard-headed commonsense of the Unionist population will come to the fore and make the best of the situation. The positions would now be reversed. The Nationalist population would now have the protection of the Irish army. Regretfully I cannot say that would be of much help if one is to judge by their performance at Ballinamore where a few untrained IRA men out-witted and out-manoeuvered them.

Myth No. 3. The British army in Ireland is a peace-keeping force.

Outside the Six Counties the British like to portray the role of the army as that of a kind of fairy godmother protecting the innocent, seeing them safely to their homes at night, if not exactly tucking them into bed. One young British officer in a military bar said to me: 'We are in Northern Ireland to try to preserve some form of civilised living.' I think he was hurt when I told him with some derision that very few people in Northern Ireland would accept that view and indeed most would laugh at its naïvety.

Unfortunately the record of these men who have been sent to keep the peace in the North is nothing to be proud of. Their treatment of the Nationalist population is only marginally better than the treatment of the inhabitants of occupied countries by the Gestapo; arrogant, oppressive and brutal. Indeed one can frequently see such items of graffiti on Belfast walls as *Nazi Brits Go Home.* They do not worry too much about who they shoot as long as it can be done in a publicly credible situation. Massive efforts have been made to conceal the fact *that nine out of every ten acts of violence in the Six Counties have been committed by the security forces.* This is something our politicians and our media have failed to emphasise. Since the troubles began the Six County security forces have shot down hundreds of unarmed men, women and children. They have maimed more than one thousand, used plastic bullets which they are forbidden to use in England but allowed to use against the Irish. One sergeant when asked by his superior officer if he would have any problems in shooting Catholics or Protestants answered, 'No sir, just so long as provided they're Irish.' In their house-to-house searches they have beaten up women, some pregnant, kicked little children, smashed furniture and family pictures, dragged young men and girls by the hair out into the streets. In 1973 an army lieutenant was quoted in the *Manchester Guardian* as saying:

> You know when we were in Ballymurphy. . . we had these people really fed up with us, really terrified. I understand what refugees must feel like in Vietnam. . . after every shooting incident we would order fifteen hundred houses searched – fifteen hundred!

Another officer said:

> Ski-ing or mountain climbing has got nothing on a cordon and search when you get old Snodgrass out of bed at four in the morning and you go through his house like a dose of salts.

In an interview with the same *Guardian* newspaper, a young paratrooper said:

> Although you moan about Ireland at least you're going to have a chance to shoot some bastard through the head. . . You're there to kill people and to see guys killed. . .

It is not hard to imagine the publicity these statements would get in the Irish media and the hysterical condemnation they would bring about had they been made by the IRA!

In the Ardoyne area Unionist gangs burned down Nationalist homes while the army stood with their backs to the arsonists and aimed their guns at the Nationalists. In 1974 during the Unionist strike the British army refused to take action against the Unionist intimidators. The soldiers, and indeed the RUC, told journalists that they had orders not to do so. If one ignores the official spokesmen and speaks to the rank and file most of them will tell you the hard truth. They will tell you that in the special training course they undergo prior to taking up duty in Northern Ireland it is made quite clear to them that the enemy is the Nationalist population.

It would be pleasant to say that these incidents were the exceptions but unfortunately this is normal behaviour. Their conduct has been fully documented in responsible newspapers and publications. In 1972 the New York based *International League for the Rights of Man* reported:

> Evidence exists that the British army engages in wide-spread assaults on both a random and selective basis. . . Those particularly affected are ex-internees. These are subjected to being continually arrested and frequently beaten.

A similar statement came from the London based *National Council for Civil Liberties*.

A recently published report by a group of international lawyers called *Shoot to Kill?* severely indicted the British government and the security forces in the North for their activities in the North and concluded that the Irish government would be justified in bringing an inter-state application to the European Court of Human Rights because the British government appeared to tolerate a shoot-to-kill policy by its security forces in Northern Ireland. Needless to say the present Coalition have not brought any such proceedings. Anyone caring to check for themselves should spend a few days strolling around the Nationalist areas in Belfast. Here the whole thing can be seen on the ground: Saracens firing shots into Nationalists area; houses searched where furniture is broken an smashed 'to teach these fucking Irish a lesson'; spot checks where people, including pregnant women, are put up against a street wall, searched and beaten with rifle butts. There is hardly anyone living in a Nationalist area who has not experienced this brutal harassment and this in their own country. Yet one can travel freely through the Unionist areas without seeing a British soldier. Regrettably the British army have a long string of killings to their credit and the few who ever appear in court are usually found not guilty.

As well as these units of the regular army worse still was in store for the Nationalist population in the Special Air Service, more generally known as the SAS. Whether one likes it or not these are in effect legalised terrorists. For the most part these specially trained men wear civilian clothes, travel in plain cars, carry knives, daggers, sub-machine guns and the outlawed pump-action shotguns. They are also issued with a special glove, steel-lined and mailed, so that it can tear a man's face to pieces. One of its prime functions according to *British Army Land Operations Manual* is to set up special 'assassination parties'. The type of individual who can be found in this force may be judged from the methods used when they stormed the Iranian embassy in London. Having felled one man with the butt of a rifle they then shot him twenty-five times. They put twelve bullets into another man and twenty bullets into yet another. Commenting on this operation Margaret Thatcher said it made her 'proud to be British'. For once she surely spoke the truth.

In the North they operate mostly along the Border and especially in South Armagh. Their object is (1) to kill on sight and without trial suspected IRA leaders and (2) to terrorise the Nationalist population by torture, blackmail and at times even murder. In one month thirty young civilians were shot from passing cars by the SAS. So bad were their activities that the Civil Rights Association had to publish a booklet called *What to do if the SAS Shoot at You*. One of the more chilling parts reads:

> Providing you are alive when the shooting stops, pretend to be dead until the squad moves away, otherwise they might try to finish the job. If there is any army post nearby do not worry. It will not be manned or if it is the occupants will be busy writing press statements to say that no military personnel were involved in the shooting.

One of the most frightening books ever written on Northern Ireland has been written by two priests, Fathers Denis Faul and Raymond Murray, entitled *SAS Terrorism – The Assassin's Glove*. This is a history of the atrocities committed by this unit in the Six Counties backed up by signed, witnessed statements, photographs and maps. Reading it makes one almost lose faith in human nature.

One member of the SAS told journalists in Dublin that his

job was to cause explosions in Northern Ireland so that the IRA would be blamed. Seemingly he spoke out of turn. Shortly afterwards he was shot dead by his erstwhile colleagues.

One cannot rule out the possibility that there is a certain amount of experimentation being carried out by the British army in the Six Counties. This is the first campaign of its kind in a developed society which is a part of what is supposed to be a democracy. New techniques, new methods and new weapons are being tried out. All these, or some of the more successful may be used later in riot-control in Britain itself. In this sense the military lessons to be learned might well be seen to be worth the cost in lives and money. The callousness of such a policy is by no means outside the orbit of the British ruling classes. In their eyes the Irish can always be used as cannon fodder.

I think I could not be accused of exaggerating if I suggest that there is much more than a doubt hanging over the activities of the British army in the Six Counties and if the forces of law and order do not administer justice and are themselves guilty of criminal acts then one can begin to understand how young men are forced to resort to violence.

These massive attempts by the British to bluff the world as to their intentions in the Six Counties have also suceeded among many Irish politicians. However, Haughey does not seem to have been fooled and he has continually shown that he has grasped the realities and is prepared to act with such courage and integrity that the British are none too happy at the prospect of his return to power.

We should not be deluded into the quaint belief that the British interest in our country is only centred on the occupied Six Counties. The far-reaching plans she has drawn up for the defence of her own people includes the entire Republic as well as the Six Counties. She wants the whole of Ireland to be the front firing line in case a nuclear attack is mounted on her from submarines in the Atlantic. She badly needs bases all along our western seaboard to give adequate warning of the approach of cruise missiles so that they could be destroyed over the Atlantic and so save the destruction of British cities. Regrettably the media have not drawn the attention of the Irish people to what is most likely to happen to them in such an event. One must assume that the Russian general in charge of this operation would not be a fool. If he saw in our bases a danger to the success of his missiles he would destroy these bases at once. Translated into people that means the slaughter of a possible 250,000 Irish men, women and children in the first days of a war – and all this to protect British cities.

This kind of thinking explains the strong attacks on Irish neutrality made by British politicians and indeed some unthinking Irishmen. Commenting on this a perceptive *Sunday Press* columnist said:

> He (Britain's Defence Minister Heseltine) wants Ireland to abandon neutrality and join NATO. . . Few would accuse Mr Heseltine of being over concerned with the well-being of Ireland and the Irish people. He simply wants cannon fodder and the use of this part of Ireland for NATO exercises. . . he does not like our attachment to neutrality because this does not suit Britain.

Of course one cannot condemn the British for this. They are merely out to protect their own people. If condemnation is to be indulged in then surely it should be directed at the Irish politicians who have allowed themselves to be so fooled.

There are two possible ways in which the British domination of Ireland might be brought about. The first, an actual armed invasion of the Republic, is unlikely, although there is a serious school of thought, particularly in the Six Counties, which holds that the British are trying to ferment a civil war in the Republic, and this could then be used as an excuse for invasion. This theory cannot be dismissed out of hand. If they thought world opinion would let them away with it they would not hesitate. During the Second World War they had a division ready in Northern Ireland to invade us. As well their plans provided for the use of poison gas against us in certain circumstances. It would be the height of folly to think they would show us any mercy. They never have.

The second way they can hold sway over us is by having a government in the Republic sympathetic to British aims and prepared to go a long way to meet British demands. This does not seem to them a very formidable task. They were particularly happy some years ago with the Fianna Fáil government who granted almost every demand they made and, of course, they are delighted with the performance of the present Coalition.

Ultimately the Republican conscience of Fianna Fáil rebelled. A new leader, Charles J. Haughey, was elected. Many hoped that Haughey would put an end at once to this collaboration with the British. He did not do so and for this he must be seriously faulted. He has never explained why but some political commentators believe that he was unsure of the loyalty of all the party, since many had little or no ideals, and that he set party unity as his initial task, hoping that when this was achieved he could then deal with the British. This may well have been a grave error.

Another school of thought holds that if he came to grips with the British first and showed his mettle party unity would come easier. This is hard to assess. It is true that he did not have a united party of Republicans behind him in the sense that both De Valera and Lemass had. In De Valera's long and bitter struggle with the British the Fianna Fáil party, composed of civil war veterans, were behind him to a man. Here I stress the word 'Republican' because Nationalist ideals within Fianna Fáil were somewhat dormant and indeed there were some within the party who would be more at home with Fine Gael. Nevertheless his weakness in allowing a man like George Colley to have such a say in the appointments to Justice and Defence, is a major black mark against him.

There are those who say that Haughey's lowest point was the arms trial. I do not think so. The arms trial may well have been his highest point, and when the full history of the real reason behind this shameful trial comes to be written Haughey may well emerge as one of the outstanding Irishman of the period. But he did have a bad low when he placed his trust in Thatcher and the British during Bobby Sands' hunger-strike. The result of that misplaced trust was to have far-reaching effects not only on the lives of the hunger-strikers but on the future of Mr Haughey himself. When world leaders tried to intercede for Bobby Sands' life Thatcher was able to refuse by saying that she had the full support of the Fianna Fáil government. More than thirty special envoys were dispatched from London to various countries to hammer home that point. Another result of that mistake was that Haughey lost an election where he could have had an overall majority and thus spared the country the terrible consequences of Coalition government. Once again the British won.

Unlike FitzGerald, however, one of the statesman-like qualities Haughey has is his ability to learn from his mistakes – and to learn fast. This in any politician is a tremendous character trait. It is most unlikely he will ever be tricked by British treachery again.

For their part the British now realise that they will not succeed in finding a Fianna Fáil government under Charles Haughey to be subservient to their wishes, but it is a different proposition with Fine Gael. Here, they believe, they will have very few problems and it seems as if the track record proves them correct.

The Fine Gael party started off in 1922 as the pro-Treaty party. As chairman of the Provisional Government Michael Collins was *de facto* the leader of this party but he was skilfully manoeuvred out of this position because of his continued Republicanism. The Treaty to him was only a means to a full Thirty-Two County Republic. Both Michael Collins and Eoin O'Duffy made their intentions clear to Liam Lynch when they told him: 'The Treaty would give breathing space, allow the army to equip; then we could declare war when ever a suitable opportunity came.' But the entire 'stepping stone' idea died with the mysterious shooting of Collins at Béal-na-Bláth, and the new pro-Treaty party, under the leadership of W. T. Cosgrave, became a Commonwealth party under the name of Cumann na nGaedheal, later to become Fine Gael. As a young student in Galway university I heard W. T. Cosgrave state: 'It is the aim of our party that Ireland should be a good member of the British Commonwealth.' I have no real evidence to show that they ever moved from that position. As far as I can see they are still the Commonwealth party. Their actions since they were founded surely point to this. They yielded on the Boundary Commission in 1925, and gave away Six Counties instead of Three as agreed between Lloyd George and Michael Collins.

They accepted this Boundary Agreement and had it registered internationally, thereby becoming partners with the British in suppressing the Nationalists of the North. Today they do not like to be reminded of this since the logical conclusion to be drawn is that they are co-partners in all the crime that has been committed in the North since then and share equally with the British responsibility for the 3,000 deaths in Northern Ireland.

They opposed the removal of the Oath of Allegiance to King

George V. They opposed the Constitution of 1937 which made the Twenty-Six counties a Republic in all but name. They gave the most milk and water support to neutrality in 1939 – but even there it was a qualified support. General Mulcahy made it quite clear that they disagreed with De Valera when he stated that he would resist a British invasion in arms. All in all, they have never, as far as I am aware, deviated from the Commonwealth idea, if we except a brief period in 1948 when they did so to hold on to office and upstage De Valera.

I am not criticising them for these policies – this is a democracy and they have a right to pursue what policies they like – but I think they should come out openly and tell the public that they are a Commonwealth party and they believe in the dominance of Britain over Ireland and let the people decide. It is unfair to the Irish electorate to say they are Nationalists while their actions tend to distort the very foundation of the national ethic.

But whatever they are the British are delighted with them. They see Garret FitzGerald, not as a prime minister of Ireland, but as a mere administrator, a kind of county manager of a British County Council. They believe that both Coalition parties are mere county councillors who should do as they are told and ask no questions, and that they should run Ireland with a watchful eye on British interests.

Are these British beliefs correct? Is there some substance behind them? To answer these questions one must ask two supplementary questions: Have Fine Gael ever really stood up to the British? Or has their track record been of compliance?

Unfortunately for our people the answer to both these supplementary questions is reasonably clear. I know of no case over the past few years where Fine Gael stood up to the British on a matter of national principle and all the evidence publicly available tends to suggest that compliance with British wishes is the order of the day.

They propose a national crusade to remove two articles in our Constitution which will have the effect of telling the world that Britain owns the Six Counties and not us.

They have very correctly condemned the regime in the Six Counties as unacceptable and indeed criminal at times, yet they spend one million pounds of Irish taxpayer's money every day supporting that regime. It is not that they are indifferent to the plight of the one million Irish people at home who are below the poverty line. It is that British military interests have priority. If there is any money left over having satisfied British needs then it will be given to the Irish.

Although they successfully and courageously prosecuted the security forces in the Six Counties for torture and inhuman conduct they collaborated fully with these forces along the Border to a degree that one wonders at times if our gardaí have been integrated into the RUC.

They have shamefully allowed the extradition of young Irishmen to this criminal regime despite long and honoured legal precedent, thus making clear to the world that the Six Counties is a British state and not an Irish one.

The list of collaboration and compliance is endless. It seems as if the slightest whim of the British is granted without question. But perhaps worst of all is the absolute contempt which the British show towards the Fine Gael-Labour leadership. The British have publicly insulted, humiliated and poured indignity on these Irishmen to a degree far greater than they ever did with any other political leaders. The response of our elected Irish leaders has been to lick their wounds, fall on their knees and beg a little mercy and a crumb from the table, and come back again and again for more insults. The all time low in the history of Ireland, including the Act of Union and the Famine, was reached at the summit meeting in November 1984 when Margaret Thatcher kicked and booted Garret FitzGerald, and rubbed his nose in the political mire in front of the entire watching world and in doing so humiliated the Irish nation to a degree never before accomplished – and FitzGerald once again dropped to his knees, made humble obeisance and accepted it all without a murmur. Indeed if anything, he praised Thatcher and when he had wiped off the British spittle, he told us what wonderful progress he was making with her. This incident more than any other highlights the appalling political ineptness of FitzGerald and his advisors and the wise far-seeing statesmanship of Charles Haughey upon whom fell the mantle of giving expression to the angry humiliated feelings of the Irish people when their elected Taoiseach would not do so. Let us take a brief look at this incident.

Very few people in the country took the Forum as seriously

as those who were part of it. The Irish public have long memories and they had not forgotten Lloyd George's famous Convention of 1917, a red herring designed to confuse the real issues, and from which Sinn Féin were excluded. Was our Forum a red herring? There is a substantial body of serious opinion in the country who would say that it was primarily designed to boost John Hume's position in the North and only in the second place did it concern itself with presenting a consensus of views as to how justice, and consequently peace, could be brought to the Six Counties. If there is substance in that viewpoint then Fitz-Gerald added yet another major blunder to his already long list of misjudgments in relation to the Six Counties. What does, however, seem somewhat grotesque was the fact that pro-British and pro-Unionist elements, who refused to renounce violence, were welcomed and given a full hearing, while pro-Irish and pro-Nationalist elements who refused to renounce violence were denied a hearing. No wonder so many of the Irish public saw the Forum as an ill-conceived, badly operated exercise.

Yet it would be unfair to dismiss it as a total write-off. Despite the imbalance of its establishment composition it did issue a report of some merit recommending a unitary state as the best chance of bringing justice and peace to the country as a whole. Any child on the Falls Road could have told them that, and so spared the Irish taxpayer the one million pounds the Forum is reputed to have cost. But then nobody from the Falls Road was given a hearing!

This document, so far removed from the ideals of the founders of the State, was humbly offered, with due respect to the British who rejected it out of hand and poured contempt on its contents. It is doubtful if Thatcher even read it. Again any child in a primary school history class could have foreseen that result. The British are not interested in justice or peace in the Six Counties. They are an army of occupation, who want military bases for their own defence, and if, due to new technological advances they no longer need those bases, they will leave. But not until then – and all the Summits, Forums and Crusades will not alter that fact one iota.

So much has been written about Garret FitzGerald's appalling performance at the 1984 Summit with Thatcher that one can only wonder how he has lasted as leader of Fine Gael. She treated him like dirt, rubbed his nose in the gutter, and in doing so humiliated the whole Irish nation. There was nothing unusual in such treatment of the Irish by an English prime minister, but what was unprecedented in the course of Irish history was FitzGerald's acceptance of it without a murmur of protest. Indeed like the errant school boy he took his caning and returned meekly to the dunce's corner of the political classroom. But it was even worse than that. He told the Irish people that this degrading summit was successful and worthwhile. In the Cork area there was a story going the rounds – apocryphal no doubt – that someone asked a West Cork farmer what he now thought of FitzGerald. The farmer replied: 'The trouble with him is that when Thatcher threw the piss in his face he really thought it was champagne!'

Those of us who hoped that he would stand up to the British insults in the same way as De Valera, Seán Lemass or John A. Costello would, were sadly disappointed as were so many prominent members of his own party who saw in his senseless and doctrinaire words what one of those supporters described as 'all froth and no porter'.

But the picture was not all gloom. The honour of the Irish people was to some degree salvaged by Charles Haughey, who in a most statesmanlike speech in Dáil Éireann made clear to the British, and particularly to Thatcher, that the Irish people still had a voice. This speech is so important that it is worth looking at in some detail.

He began by putting the entire Summit in its real true context devoid of the public whitewashing attempted by the Coalition:

> Yesterday's Summit between the Taoiseach and the British Prime Minister was one of the most depressing and humiliating meetings between heads of government that I can ever recall. Yesterday the report of the New Ireland Forum, the carefully considered view of the democratic nationalist representatives of three quarters of all the Irish was unceremoniously and aggressively rejected by the British Prime Minister, and this rejection was accepted without a whisper of remonstration from the Taoiseach. There can be no escape from the dismal fact that constitutional nationalism took a beating yesterday and the evasiveness and incoherence of the Taoiseach in his press conference afterwards served only to accentuate that humiliating reality.

He dealt harshly with the propaganda being put about at home by Fine Gael – propaganda which aimed at showing that a great break-through was about to be made in relation to Northern Ireland when in fact there was no break-through. The age-old Britain had shown her teeth once more. Mr Haughey commented:

> In an interview with the *Irish Times* the Taoiseach was claiming that the British and Irish governments have a similar analysis of what the problem is. It is now quite obvious that there is no basis for that claim. It was fraudulent. . . All those media manipulators around the Taoiseach have discovered the hard way that floating stories in the domestic media can be counter-productive. The fostering of illusions about British interest, about British goodwill and about British receptiveness, about twenty-year treaties, about personal preferences, where did it all lead? – to a cold calculated reprimand for both master and servants. . . No one is taken in by the suggestion that there is something more of significance to come. . . The new Secretary of State, Mr Hurd spelled out the British view when he said that no amount of Summit meetings would solve the problems facing the parties in the North. . . What is the point of another Summit if the Taoiseach is going to be walked on all over once again?

In a courageous and statesman-like way Haughey spoke for the Irish people as a whole when he said:

> The official voice of Nationalist Ireland was so muffled yesterday as to be inaudible. The British Prime Minister was direct, intransigent and brutally frank. Let me also be direct and frank. We who represent Nationalist Ireland do not accept the rejection of the New Ireland Forum Report and with it all the hopes and aspirations of the majority of the Irish people. We will continue to fight at home and abroad for the only solution that will bring lasting peace and justice to this land of ours.

And commenting on the disastrous role played by Garret FitzGerald in this humiliation of the Irish people, Mr Haughey had this to say:

> On a previous occasion in this house I sought to warn the present Taoiseach about the danger inherent in his approach and attitude to Anglo-Irish relations, both in its personal-and its official aspects. My warning had no effect and the Taoiseach continued along his

foolish way till it brought him finally to yesterday's humiliation. . .
Events have shown this behaviour to have been damaging and
detrimental to a deadly extent. International relations, international discussions, international negotiations, are not kindergar-
ten matters, nor are they conducted as if they were some kind of
amicable parlour game. . . it is difficult to comprehend why the
outcome of yesterday's Summit took the brutal form it did. There
can, unfortunately, be only one explanation. The British Prime
Minister and the British government have settled on a clear and
definite policy in regard to Northern Ireland, and the position the
Northern Ireland problem should occupy in Anglo-Irish relations.

They have gone right back to the old position that the Six Counties of Northern Ireland are to be regarded as an integral part of
the United Kingdom, a territory over which British sovereignty is
to be maintained and that the Unionist position in it is inviolate
and untouchable. After all the comings and goings, and accom-
modating statements and actions, after all the ingratiation we came
right back yesterday to the old sterile negative policy.

And in a scathing attack on Garret FitzGerald's blundering,
which found echoes of approval throughout the whole country,
not least amongst the ranks of Fine Gael and Labour, Haughey
said:

To the Taoiseach I say: You have led this country into the greatest
humiliation in recent history. You have failed ignominiously in an
area of vital national interest. Because of your incompetence, mis-
judgment and ineffectiveness you have done grievous damage to
our national political interests and our pride. History will record
that it would have been better if your visit to Chequers had never
taken place.

In the great tradition of De Valera and Lemass, Haughey, by
this speech, saved the national pride and the national dignity.
He made it quite clear to the British that the spirit of the old
Fianna Fáil was still alive and well, and that, despite a regrettable
interruption covering a period of years in the doldrums, the
grass roots had never really lost soul.

To translate these noble and worthy sentiments into action
when he comes face to face with the British will be a task calling
into play all his extensive resources. They will try every known
trick to vilify him, blackmail him and even cajole him with
flattery. They will not hesitate to use their good friends in the

USA and the Vatican to help them. The toughness with which he can stand up to the British and ignore their threats and flattery will mark his place for ever in Irish history.

3: The British Secret Service in Ireland

If you wish to preserve your secret wrap it up in frankness.
– ALEXANDER SMITH

I hope the Irish may always be disunited. The great art is to keep them so.
– SIR ROBERT PEEL

You must stop your inquiries. . . You will be helping the enemy.
– LORD CHALFONT to journalists investigating Kim Philby.

I have no reason to conclude that Mr Philby has at any time betrayed the interests of this country. . .
– HAROLD MacMILLAN M.P.

What is all this poppycock you have sent me about isolating and quarantining Nasser? Can't you understand I want Nasser murdered.
– SIR ANTHONY EDEN to Foreign Office Official

A chapter on the role of the British secret service in Ireland may seem, at first sight, out of place in a book concerned with the statesmanship of Charles Haughey, but a closer examination will show it to be a major ingredient in any such study. The British deserve full marks for having, very early on, detected something unique in Haughey. Almost from the outset of his career they seem to have surmised, that of all the younger generation of Irish politicians, he was the one most likely to be a stumbling block to the overall British plan to keep Ireland a weak state in the shadow of Britain. It may well be that from a very early date they put him under surveillance and began to build up a file to be used against him, if and when it was in their interests to do so. Special attention was directed towards his private life so as to smear and, indeed, blackmail him if they could find anything that would serve this purpose to good effect. British agents live in a world where truth and honesty hardly exist. Lies, falsehoods, blackmail and even murder are their stock-in-trade. They serve their masters faithfully without moral scruple.

In order to get a clear view of how the British secret service works it is important to distinguish between the two main arms, MI5 and MI6. MI5 concerns itself with matters within Britain itself while MI6 is engaged in activities outside the country. MI5 is seen as a somewhat inept organisation of comparatively recent origin – indeed it is said that it was Fenian activity in Britain that brought it into being. Again and again it has been humiliated and out-witted, not only by the IRA, but by the KGB as well. But not so MI6. This is a superb force with hundreds of years experience behind it. It has effectively penetrated all corners of the world and is largely responsible for Britain's political successes in that it was the main force in creating in each country the climate necessary to bring these successes about. In his standard work *The Intelligence War*, Colonel William V. Kennedy tells us that:

> The great strength of SIS (MI6) lies in its world wide sources developed during the period of the British Empire and retained in the commonwealth system and in other more informal connections maintained as the former colonies became independent.

The operative words here are 'more informal connections maintained'. Translated into the language of *realpolitik* this could be taken to mean that when the British left each colony a few friends remained behind. How many did they leave after them in Ireland? It is not within the scope of this book to answer this question but one cannot help suspecting that in the early years of the State, they were not entirely blameless in the shooting of Michael Collins, Séan Hales and many of the notorious seventy-seven executions.

Closely allied to MI6 is the Government Communications Headquarters at Cheltenham, commonly known as GCHQ. It is unfortunate that lack of vigilance on the part of Irish governments has resulted in the bizarre state of affairs in which these people can now listen in to virtually every telephone call in Ireland. This includes telephone calls by Mr Haughey, calls between cabinet ministers, calls between our Department of Foreign Affairs and embassies abroad. The secrets of Irish institutions are now an open book to the British if reliance is placed on the telephone. Needless to say there is no reciprocation. We do not have the means of finding out what they are saying or thinking.

There are quite a lot of misconceptions about the precise role of MI6 in Ireland. Whenever the word 'spy' or 'agent' is mentioned it conjures up visions of Bond-like figures stealing important state documents or photo-copying highly confidential military plans. These kind of operations are only a very small part of their work – indeed in so far as Ireland is concerned a minimal activity.

Here in this country their principle job is to mould and condition Irish politicians, the Irish media and the Irish people to *think like the British* and in this way to make sure that not only is nothing effective done to unite the country, but that the country will be favourably disposed towards British strategic interests in the Republic itself.

They use every known means of persuasion, whether ethical or not; manipulation of the media, flattery of journalists, civil servants, police, army and judiciary. Included, too, in their repertoire are somewhat more unsavoury methods: torture, blackmail, robbery and even murder itself. No holds are barred and all of these methods have been used in Ireland at one time or another over the past two decades.

A fundamental part of their plan has been to bring into disrepute in the minds of the Irish people the very concepts of Republicanism, of freedom, of love of country. This they have achieved in a manner most brilliant. They did not fall into the trap of attacking Republicanism openly because they knew that if you scratch an Irishman deeply enough you will find a Republican. Instead they used a far more subtle method: equate the concept of Republicanism, of freedom, of love of Ireland with the IRA, and by bringing the IRA into disrepute these concepts were *ipso facto* brought into disrepute. It was an outstanding success. By drawing a distinction between the political ideals of the IRA and the methods used to promulgate these ideals they were able to portray Republicanism and Nationalism as the attributes and characteristics of terrorists and gunmen. In order to promulgate that part of their policy they themselves carried out a number of bombings and murders both North and South of the Border in circumstances where it was likely that the IRA would be blamed. It is also suspected that some of the more revolting and irresponsible killings carried out by the IRA, such as the Harrods bombing, were prompted by members of MI6 who had infiltrated the organisation, and in this way bring it into disrepute.

The Fianna Fáil government of the 1970s, the present Fine Gael-Labour government and the church seem to have fallen for this deception. Most of the Irish media, unfortunately, did not show any great awareness in investigating and exposing it. It was one of the most brilliant successes of MI6. They skilfully succeeded, with of course the help of many Irishmen, in identifying in the minds of the Irish people the notion of patriotism with that of murder or violence. This of course produced the extraordinary phenomena of today when many people are afraid to stand up for patriotism and self-determination in case they might be labelled anarchists and terrorists. Sections of the media have been so skilfully manipulated that many of them when referring to the IRA call them 'gunmen' while the British SAS are 'soldiers'. They refer to children murdered by plastic bullets as 'killed' but if a British soldier is killed he is 'callously gunned down'. The SAS, known the world over as comprising for the most part of highly paid terrorists, never 'murder' anybody – they only 'shoot in the course of duty'. Watch a typical television programme on the funeral of a member of the Northern security forces. In most cases the camera will linger on the tear-stained faces of his widow and children. There will be no concentrating on the Union Jack on the coffin. If, on the other hand, the funeral is one of a Republican paramilitary the camera is unlikely to linger on the weeping widow or children but instead is more likely to concentrate on masked men with guns. In both cases the effect produced is revulsion for Republican actions.

So brilliant has this whole operation been that large sections of the Irish people are now ashamed of the Easter Rebellion and of the Anglo-Irish War, while the saddest part of all is that on most issues our Coalition government are seeing things from the British viewpoint. They too are ashamed of our struggle for freedom in the past.

Here it might be worth reflecting on the perceptive words of Des Wilson in his book *An End to Silence*.

What the British government describes as terrorism by thugs and criminals is in reality the desperate response of good people who believe that there are limits to the insults which they can be expected to endure. One should not under-estimate the moral quality of people who take up arms and it is well to reflect that, broadly speaking, the only body of people in Northern Ireland who have taken up arms for money are the British forces.

It does not seem, however, that Haughey has been misled by this propaganda. Like De Valera in the late 1920s and early 1930s he has consistently voiced the right to total freedom and self determination and is not ashamed of Pearse and his followers. It is intriguing to observe that when he does express these fundamental ideals, sections of the media turn on him and accuse him of playing the 'green card', being out of date, of damaging the will-o'-the-wisp thing known as 'Anglo-Irish relations'. It seems as if his failure to see things through the red lenses of the British is a capital sin in their eyes.

One of the latest notions being floated is that he will lose votes if he does not abandon his national policy. Over and over history has proven that this is sheer nonsense. Only a minority of the population are anti-nationalist and no matter what he does he will never win their votes. This notion says that he should forget about national pride and concentrate on purely economic issues, but economic success is based on national pride. Business ability can be bought – love of country cannot. 'The morale is to the physical as three is to one,' said Napoleon. All world history proves that only when a national spirit is high can an economy improve. MI6 would like to dull that idea. In making people forget the national ideal they would see themselves a long way on the road to success.

But if one does not respond to the softly-softly approach, MI6 has other means in its repertoire. Vilification is one of these means. In my book *Operation Brogue* I have shown how effectively the British have used this weapon in Ireland. If you cannot buy a man off or win him over then try to destroy him: Parnell, Casement, Pearse, Connolly, Collins, De Valera, Lemass and now Haughey. This list of names reads like a great roll of honour in Irish history. When, in my book *Operation Brogue*, I suggested that the British secret service were largely behind this campaign I was accused of being paranoid, crazy and sensational.

I was, however, able to console myself by the fact that virtually every writer on secret service matters has been given similar treatment. All those great British writers who tried to expose the infiltration of British institutions by the KGB had the same accusations levelled against them. But time and events proved that they were on the right track and were far from being paranoid. In my own case I was intrigued to read a paragraph in the biography of Sir Maurice Oldfield, head of MI6, which confirmed my view. This biography was published four months *after* my book. The paragraph reads as follows:

> But MI6's main success (in Ireland) was in establishing agents inside the garda, the Irish army and government departments. One of the most vital informants was a senior garda officer who (up to 1981 at least) was still in the force. He had not only provided information on the IRA but on the activities of the former Irish premier, Mr Haughey, and other prominent political figures.

This paragraph shows that Haughey was a prime target and it is reasonable to assume that the information given by this senior officer (and how many others?) provided a basis for the campaign that was to follow. In itself this is a very serious matter but the other implications it contains are far more serious. Though it was not given very much prominence the above paragraph was quoted in sections of the Irish media when the book appeared. Yet to my knowledge the Fine Gael Coalition never commented on it. This is but one piece in a mysterious jig-saw, the pattern of which would seem to show that Fine Gael have either closed their eyes to the activities of the British secret service in Ireland, or are ineptly unaware of them. The reasonable requests made by Joseph Ainsworth, Seán Doherty, TD and Michael Woods, TD to hold a public inquiry into the activities of the police have been refused. Ainsworth's investigation into the leaking of government information was stopped. Seán Doherty was engaged in a full scale investigation of the activities of the British secret service when there was change of government. This investigation was also stopped. It is not unreasonable for the ordinary person to ask if Fine Gael are afraid of something emerging which might be detrimental to themselves. Surely it would not be too much to ask them to make a public statement which might clarify these issues. It is

not hard to imagine the outcry in Britain if there were evidence
to show that Irish intelligence agents had penetrated the police
force, army and government departments in London. This whole
attitude of Fine Gael to the British secret service is central to
any study of the leadership of Charles Haughey, in so far as it
shows the sheer enormity of the task of cleaning up the dreadful
mess in the sensitive Department of Justice.

In *Operation Brogue* I drew attention to the methods used by
the British secret service in moulding journalists, writers, civil
servants, judges etc. such as flattery, false praise, entertaining,
wining and dining. I wrote with some slight trepidation as I was
not quite sure of the extent of these activities. Since then I have
found out that I only touched the tip of the iceberg. These
endeavours are widespread. They affect every strata of Irish life
in ways that I had not comprehended. For example, it never
occurred to me that they would have infiltrated the banks. I
learned later that indeed they had. Apart from subtly trying to
influence who gets credit facilities they keep a watchful eye on
the personal accounts of people in the media. If it appeared that
any such person might be in financial difficulty word could be
passed out and that person might very well be offered some
lucrative freelance assignment worth far more than the going
rate in financial terms. Thus a convert to the 'decent' British
point of view could be won over. I am now certain that they
have penetrated every worth-while corner of Irish life and that
vast sums of money are being spent in this area – sums far greater
than I at first thought. I also found out that not only MI6 were
involved in this work but also many British business interests,
organisations, agencies etc. Every area of Irish life seems to
have been thoroughly penetrated in one way or another.

When relationships between two countries are good there is
generally little need for spies. Indeed the secret service organisations work closely together, such as is the case with Britain
and the USA. This general rule does not apply to Ireland despite
the fact that the relationship between a Fine Gael Ireland and
a Thatcher Britain are excellent, even though it is the relationship of servant and master.

There are two factors in Ireland which militate against this
rule. The first is the unpredictable revolutionary spirit of the
people which has surfaced again and again over hundreds of

years. A perfect example of this unpredictability might be the
state of Ireland at the turn of the century. It appeared at that
time that British domination over Ireland was total and complete. Yet within a few years there was a major revolution followed by a bloody war which ended in the separation of a large
part of Ireland from England. The British, therefore, see the
Irish as untrustworthy and liable to turn on them at any moment.
In such a climate they must operate their own secret service.
The second reason is that the British cannot completely trust
the Irish police force. While large sections of this force have
been brainwashed to the point where they are pro-British, the
bulk of the gardaí are Irish at heart. Most of them are the sons
or grandsons of men who fought and died fighting the Black-and-
Tans – and they have long memories. In order to carry out their
over-all plan the British must infiltrate the gardaí, as they have
done unfortunately with some success. Many incidents prove this.

The Crinnion case is just one example known to most people.
Here a sergeant in the most sensitive inner recesses of the Irish
special branch was caught red handed passing on state secrets
to the British. But Crinnion was only a tiny fish in the pool. The
big fish got away and for all one knows they are still with us and
still working for the British.

The bugging of Seamas Mallon's hosts, the Moynas at Kilbar-
rack, was another example – one where, according to the most
recent and reliable accounts, active British secret service agents,
assisted by sympathetic members of the Irish police force actually
installed the bug. Indeed, cases have been known where the
Irish secret service, laughable as it is, tipped off British agents
here when local gardaí, not in the know, became suspicious of
these agents.

Another well known case was that of a British army officer
who posed as an arms dealer, came to Ireland and offered arms
to Republican interests. He hoped to ingratiate himself so as to
find out the intentions of the Irish government regarding the Six
Counties. He was eventually unmasked, not by the Irish Special
Branch, but by an army officer, Captain James Kelly, who was
rewarded for his brilliant and patriotic work by being arrested
and put on trial in the disgraceful arms trial.

The case of the Littlejohn brothers is probably the best-known
of all. They were British secret agents convicted of a bank rob-

bery of £67,000 in Dublin which was being carried out as part of their duty. One of the brothers freely admitted that he was sent here on an assassination mission.

The astonishing revelations of Captain Fred Holroyd did not, for some reason, engage the attention of the Irish media to the extent that its importance warranted. In Britain, however, the courageous and brilliant journalist and writer Duncan Campbell wrote a series of articles in the *New Statesman* based on Captain Hoyroyd's revelations. Mr Campbell starts his series:

> Captain Holroyd was an intelligence specialist in Northern Ireland for nearly two years. The details of his allegations have been checked over six months. We have spoken to eye-witnesses and others personally involved in Holroyd's reports. These activities range, says Holroyd, from the disreputable to the entirely illegal – and were conducted on *both sides of the Irish border* (italics mine).

Despite efforts to smear him Holroyd was held in the highest esteem by his superiors and was described by an Assistant Chief Constable, who was in charge of the RUC's anti-terrorist campaign as 'a man of unquestionable loyalty, outstanding courage with a devotion to duty that one looks for but rarely finds today.'

A lot of Holroyd's revelations dealing with activities in the Six Counties have a very direct bearing on affairs in the Republic.

Captain Holroyd worked in close liaison with Captain Robert Nairac, an alumnus of the Benedictine College at Ampleforth and a friend of Cardinal Hume. Nairac was little better than a professional murderer, and he told Holroyd how he carried out a political assassination *south of the border*.

The victim was John Green, aged 27, who had escaped from Long Kesh Concentration Camp, and was at the time living in Monaghan. Nairac and two others crossed the Border into the South and went straight to a farmer's house where Green had been staying. They knew the exact time to go – the time when the owner left to attend to a neighbour's cow as he had been doing at the same hour for more than a month. They broke down the door and Nairac, according to his own admission, personally emptied his gun into the body of Green. Nairac then did something so bizarre that one is reminded of the Nazis. He took a Polaroid picture of the blood-stained body of Green from the waist up. The IRA eventually caught up with Nairac and executed him. Languishing in Portlaoise Jail today is a young Irishman convicted by a non-jury court of killing Nairac. Should he have been jailed or should he be given a medal? If he were an English soldier who had done a similar act, he would probable find a place on the Queen's Honours List, as indeed did some of those who were responsible for torture and even murder.

The chilling thing about this is the ease with which MI6 killers can come south of the Border and murder Irish citizens without the Irish government taking any action. Another factor is the absolute accuracy of information in the possession of these killers. They knew exactly where to go and at what precise time.

There are two versions given to explain this. The British one is that the information was passed on by an IRA informer. Another version says that the information was supplied by British agents working within the gardaí. We shall probably never know which is the true version. But what we do know is that the information was passed on by British agents, whether the gardaí or spies in the IRA, operating freely in the South and British agents carried out the murders. Again the names of those who were with Nairac are believed to be known to the Irish government, but so far no application has been made for the extradition of these killers.

Another important revelation made by Captain Holroyd was that British army units in the Six Counties arranged and planned special raids across the Border to kidnap Irish citizens who were believed to belong to the IRA. Holroyd himself was present when the army agreed to pay £500 per man to members of one team to kidnap two Irishmen living south of the Border. This particular plan went wrong as did also a second one, but what is frightening is that both sets of kidnappers were quite adamant they were assured that *British agents inside the gardaí would help them.*

British agents were also responsible for crossing the Border and attaching lethal bombs to the motor-cycle of Eugene McQuaid, a married man with five children, so that they would explode if the cycle ran into a rough patch on the road. This is actually what happened just inside the Border and McQuaid was blown to bits. A British officer picked up a fistful of McQuaid's guts and was heard to say: 'That's an end to another of you fucking bastards.'

Captain Holroyd also revealed that when he was put in charge of a number of special agents North and South three of them *were members of the gardaí*. This is again very frightening.

As far back as April 1981 the old *Sunday Tribune* published details of an authentic secret document dealing with the operation of British agents in the Republic. This was given the name Military Insurgency Operations and it covered such activities as phone tapping, opening mail, radio interception, listening devices. The document suggested that even non-political organisations such as the GAA, and the Knights of Malta, should be watched. A special surveillance was put on a west of Ireland businessman whose house was photographed so that his aerials could be examined in detail. A Limerick man and businessmen in Dundalk and Monaghan have also come under British surveillance. This type of infiltration seems to be fairly widespread throughout the country. They come pretending to be tourists or businessmen or journalists. Indeed many have been known to have faked press cards, although others are genuine journalists. One, who represented a prestigious British newspaper in Ireland had a network of contacts among Irish journalists, civil servants and politicians. He was so successful here that he was promoted to a major MI6 job in the Middle East. But the IRA's own secret service located him in Cairo and shot him. Another, a sophisticated linguist, came to Dublin posing as a tourist and spent many months doing the rounds of the Dublin pubs and trendy night clubs spotting IRA men on the run from the North. When he returned to Belfast with a lot of valuable information the IRA lured him to meet a supposed informer and as he sat in his car waiting for this man to arrive the IRA shot him.

Of course, there are many of my critics who will tempted to say that I am paranoid, that the idea of the 'friendly' British infiltrating our institutions is simply ludicrous. That, of course, is exactly the line MI6 would like people to take. It is a basic rule of MI6 that those who expose them must at all costs be discredited and ridiculed.

I am not paranoid. I know what I am talking about. What I have written about their activities in Ireland, is, if anything, understated. I have good reason to suspect that the reality is far more alarming. I am certainly amazed at how little attention has been paid to material already published. In an interview in *The*

Sunday Press with Kevin Toolis, Patrick Fitzgerald, co-author of *British Intelligence and Covert Action*, stated:

> Civil Service and media personalities are recruited in Dublin. The usual technique is to place the prospective victim under surveillance or to illegally tap his phone. MI6 look for evidence of marital disharmony, bad debts or bitterness through lack of promotion. Anything that can be used against him. They are good at it. If you can do it in Moscow then you can do it in Dublin. . . MI6 work in the Republic has been fairly successful in influencing government policy and hitting 'targets'. A reliable British security source has confirmed that the Irish media was very well penetrated.

In a most revealing series of articles in the *Irish Times* David McKittrick wrote:

> MI6 officers operate mainly from the British embassy in Dublin, transmit information on both Republican groups and political developments to London. Army intelligence personnel based in the North frequently cross the Border into the Republic to gather information and to meet agents. . . MI6 and army intelligence both maintain sizeable files on political figures in the Republic in particular Mr Haughey. Reliable sources say much attention is paid to the private lives of the politicians.

According to recent newspaper reports a dossier giving details of alleged MI6 and British military intelligence activities directed at undermining the Fianna Fáil government was sent to Mrs Thatcher by a former senior British army information officer. The title of this special dossier was *Activities Designed to Destabilise the Fianna Fáil Government* and contained vital information about the recruitment of British agents in the gardaí.

Many other excellent articles on this topic have been written by distinguished journalists over the past ten years yet there has been an amazing lack of follow-up. Government silence has also been extraordinary.

How widespread is all this? Many British criminologists believe that Britain has in all approximately 14,000 spies throughout the world. In a vitally strategic and troubled spot like Ireland it would be reasonable to assume that not less than 100 are operating here, not necessarily all full time. The few

examples I have given are but a small section of those that came
to light. For every one case that the public hears about it is
estimated that there are about twenty or thirty that never surface. What about those that have not surfaced? How many actually are there? As I have already said, I suspect the whole MI6
operation here is widespread. It affects the civil service, the
judiciary, the gardaí, the army, industry, the media and indeed
every facet of Irish life that can be used to advance and promote
British interests in Ireland. One hesitates to call us a nation of
cretins but our foolishness in swallowing all this and allowing it
to happen cannot be excused. 'The Irish are an inferior race,'
remarked Bonar Law. Was he far wrong?

I apologise for having to deal at such length with MI6 in a
book about Haughey but any study of their activities is inextric-
ably inter-woven with his whole career. Almost from the beginning of his political life he was on their 'hit' list. They threw
their whole weight and their vast financial resources behind a
massive effort to vilify and destroy him. They knew he would
not, in a final analysis, become their lickspittle and they suspected that he would take drastic steps to revive the old Fianna
Fáil spirit and lift it out of the stupor into which it had slipped.

They very nearly succeeded in destroying Haughey. Many
Irish people today were deeply alarmed when they realised how
misled they were by sections of the media and how little they
were told of the power and effectiveness of MI6 in Ireland. Any
self-respecting country would take immediate and effective steps
to put an end to this alarming state of affairs but where British
interests are concerned our present government seems
paralysed. This enormous task will now fall on Haughey's shoulders. To rout these agents and destroy them will be another
priority task. If he does not do so at once then Operation Brogue
will re-activate and this time they will do all in their power to
make sure that there will be no failure.

What steps should he take to rid the country of this cancerous
growth?

The first step ought to be the *immediate* establishment of a
counter-espionage service somewhat on the lines of the FBI.
This service should, of course, be completely independent of
the gardaí or the Department of Justice and should be answer-
able to an all-party Dáil committee under the direct control of

the Taoiseach. Because of the strong suspicion that both the gardaí and the Department of Justice are so thoroughly infiltrated by MI6 it would be much too dangerous to give them any control of, or even a say in, this organisation. Ideally they should be subservient to it.

Its directors should have immunity from dismissal except by a majority vote in the Dáil. This would help prevent a future pro-British Coalition from neutralising its functions.

The vetting of operatives for this new service would have to be of a most exacting nature. MI6 would try to infiltrate it from the beginning. It is now clear that the present system of vetting in the Irish security forces is deplorable. The Irish special branch are regarded by MI6 as little more than buffoons. They are there to be used to protect British interests in the same way the RUC use the gardaí while privately holding them in contempt.

Perhaps the most important qualification for members of this service would be a love of and dedication to their country – in other words, simple patriotism. A man who loves his country will not betray it. It has been alleged that such young men are now joining our security forces but that after a number of years they are so moulded as to hate Irish Nationalists and see the British as their friends. This, if true, is again a great tribute to MI6.

The use of the polygraph, better known as the lie dectector, might not be out of place in the vetting of recruits. The polygraph shows blood pressure, pulse beat and perspiration under questioning and reacts if a lie is being told. Apart from the valuable information it would give it would be a deterrant if members were required to take this test every two years. No doubt many 'do-gooders' will be appalled by this suggestion but if it had been obligatory for our security forces over the past fifteen years we might have saved ourselves not only a lot of trouble but a lot of lives as well.

Special care would have to be taken to ensure that training of key personnel for this new service should not be influenced by the British. Such a policy would of course eliminate training at British centres or at centres in countries who collaborate with Britain such as France, Germany, the United States and Canada. Desmond FitzGerald, father of Garret, would not agree with this advice. 'Irish officers should not be trained in a foreign

country,' he said, 'but in England or one of the dominions.'
More than once it has been publicly stated that on such training
missions some Irish have been 'got at' and even blackmailed.

It would then seem more than prudent to avoid any British
or pro-British training centres and if foreign training is necessary
then such countries as Switzerland, Austria, Libya, Sweden or
Egypt, have excellent facilities.

In the interests of national security the importance of a
counter-intelligence organisation in the present climate cannot
be over-estimated. If the cancerous burrowings of MI6 are not
stopped within the next few years we may well be totally
swamped by the British – our media British, our food British,
our industry British, our supermarkets British – the list is endless. We may find ourselves back where we were in 1916, a
nation of serfs with the lowest standard of living in Europe. If
this is allowed to happen we may well have to begin all over
again with another Pearse, another Connolly and another Easter
Week. One can now see how much the future of Ireland rests
in Haughey's hands.

4: Statesmanship in Action

Weak people never bring anything to a conclusion.
They wait for an end to come.

– TURGENEV

Power does not corrupt men; fools, however, if they get into a position
of power, corrupt power

– G. B. SHAW

Our objective is to establish a Republican government in Ireland. If that can
be done by the present methods we have we will be very pleased. But if not
we would not confine ourselves to these methods.

– SEÁN LEMASS

In order that evil may triumph it is enough that good men do nothing.

– EDMUND BURKE

In the first three chapters of this book I have dealt at length with three features of Irish life which will demand the immediate attention of Mr Haughey when he takes office: the restoration of national morale (chapter 1), standing up to the British (chapter 2), and destroying the grip of MI6 on Irish institutions (chapter 3).

If Haughey succeeds in rebuilding the national morale, in making people respect themselves as Irish men and women, he will have created a favourable climate for the achievement of all other tasks which might well be on the way to accomplishment within a few years. 'The morale is to the physical as three is to one' is the basic doctrine never to be forgotten.

In this chapter we will look at a number of other elements in the life of the country which, while not as important as the first three, are closely interlinked with all I have already written.

1.   Reform of the Civil Service

One of the mistakes we made in 1922 was that we took over the civil service as it was, lock, stock and barrel. It was a British institution which operated to suit, not Irish, but British interests. Here, more than anywhere else, we should have decolonised

and adapted our civil service to serve the needs of the Irish
people. Of course, unlike other countries who gained their freedom, we did not decolonise at all. Probably because of the commonwealth mentality of the then government we retained all
the outward trappings of our former masters: names of streets,
parks, buildings, hotels, schools etc., and we still retain many
of these marks of servitude today. The result of our failure to
decolonise the civil service in particular, was that British moulds
of practice and procedure became the standards to which we
worked. The British spirit permeated throughout and although
nearly seventy years have passed since then we have made
little headway in decolonising either our institutions or our exter
nal structures. British standards largely prevail and we tend to
look to London for inspiration and guidance rather than to look
to other countries, or indeed, think things out for ourselves.

Haughey seems to have recognised this defect when he said:

> We have often been content merely to follow British example when
> framing our economic, social and cultural policies, instead of rely-
> ing on our own creative abilities and looking to the experience of
> other European countries whose situation in many respects more
> closely resembles our own. In fact it has been argued that we have
> been most successful in those exceptional cases where we went to
> the mainland of Europe for technological assistance – like the
> Shannon Scheme, the cement industry and the development of
> peat.

One of the civil service procedures peculiarly British was that
of policy-making. Civil servants *made* decisions affecting a whole
nation and ministers endorsed these decisions, not too sure of
what they were ratifying. This was quite understandable in Britain where cabinet ministers were appointed, in a lot of cases,
because of class, privilege or wealth, even though many of them
were acknowledged dunderheads, who could hardly make an
intelligent decision, and who felt much more at home hunting,
shooting and fishing on their large estates. Thus grew up the
custom of civil service decision-making, which we in Ireland
took over without change. In this way our civil servants started
out believing that *they*, and not the elected politicians, were the
real rulers of the country. The raw young Irishmen who took
over the government in 1922 were so inexperienced and

depended so much on the knowledge of the existing civil servants that they allowed this state of affairs to continue. Even when Fianna Fáil came to power in 1932 they too were inexperienced and because of this the old moulds remained. The result was that the effective masters of the country were non-elected civil servants, cast in the British mould of thought. It has been strongly argued that this is the situation which exists today and that a great deal of our misfortunes must have their origins in this factor. Indeed in an article in *Seirbhís Phoiblí* Professor Joseph Lee suggests that one of the negative influences upon the service since its formative years was its suffusion with a British administrative ethos. Dr C. S. Andrews' book *Man of No Property* gives a fascinating account of the workings of the Irish civil service in the early days of the state, of their colonial mentality and particularly of one, who on retiring in the late 1930s, bemoaned the fact that the old regime had gone – otherwise he would have received a knighthood for his services!

Civil servants are unsuited by their education, training and by the milieu of their employment for major decision-making. The experience they are likely to acquire throughout the years is such as to encourage caution and lethargy, often to the point of absurdity.

In the same article Professor Lee states:

> The slow process of advancement requiring essentially mastery of the technique of risk avoidance, tended to leave ultimately as survivors men of considerable natural ability, extensive procedural experience, ingrained caution, narrowness of perspective and considerably muted ambition to get things done. . . The civil service in general developed strong, narrow, negative minds.

Today the young civil servant who shows initiative, enterprise, a spirit of positive decision-making and love of country is unlikely to get very far in his profession. A negative, ineffective attitude and an admiration of British standards may well serve his personal interests far better.

If we take a close look at the present-day civil service we cannot but feel a disquieting concern. In 1970 we had 218,000 civil servants. This had risen to 302,000 by 1983. Other than the kind of operation illustrated by Parkinson's Law, there seems to be no common-sense reason why this should be so. Indeed the exact opposite should be the case. The civil service spent millions of pounds over the past ten years purchasing the most highly sophisticated computers, specially designed to cut labour input. Instead labour input has inoreased. We now have one civil servant for every twelve of our population. We are gone well above the danger line, which is generally reckoned at one in twenty-five. We pay these people £6,000,000,000 every year and we pay them £200,000,000 in pensions because they do not operate a contributory pension fund like workers in the private sector. If they did the tax-payer could save £100,000,000 annually.

According to recent press reports, in every government department millions of pounds are being mispent as a result of unwise and badly researched decisions. It has been estimated that even if rudimentary business principles were put into effect by the civil service, the annual savings might well come close to £1,000,000,000.

Perhaps, if instead of being recruited on the basis of academic qualifications, they were recruited on their ability to organise, to visualise, to buy, to sell, to balance income against outgoings, they might well make a durable and lasting contribution to the welfare of this state. As long as matters are allowed to continue as they are, unfortunately, there are no valid grounds to hope for improvement, other than the hope that Mr Haughey will tackle the problem.

Many people, including the media, have not averted to one of the latest gimmicks they have used which is a great boon in evading responsibility. This gimmick is the employment of out-side consultants. This bauble was pioneered by Erskine Childers, a man whose position owed more to his name than to any ministerial ability. It is a marvellous cop-out. Whenever something of importance goes wrong consultants are called in and responsibility is thereby evaded by the civil service and put on the shoulders of anonymous consultants. Close on £10,000,000 was paid out last year to these consultants. Almost all this money could have been saved. Consultants should not be necessary to report on and decide matters of ordinary common sense.

Two thousand years ago, Cicero said:

> The budget should be balanced, the treasury should be refilled, the public debt should be reduced, the arrogance of the civil ser-

vants should be controlled. . . and the people should be forced to work and not allowed depend on the state for their support.

Is there an alternative and if so what is it? Over-all we could not do better than follow Cicero's advice. Perhaps we should view the role of the civil service as that of 'servants' and not of 'masters' – as that of executives *carrying out* and implementing government decisions rather than *making* decisions. This role would be much more in keeping with the composition, education and training of civil servants. Attached to such a role should be some form of discipline for major mistakes. It is surely unfair that the Irish taxpayer should have to put his hand in his pocket and pay up millions of pounds every time the civil service makes a blunder.

But who then would make the decisions? Obviously not, in all cases the ministers, since many are chosen for electoral reasons rather than ability, and again, it is naïve to suggest that it will ever be otherwise. Some highly successful countries use ministerial committees of three or four *outsiders* with expertise in the area of the particular ministry. This committee would be part-time and would confer weekly with the minister, make the necessary decisions which would be carried out by the civil servants, who could be penalised for dragging their feet or for any kind of obstruction.

Of course, here in Ireland, the greatest care would have to be exercised in the composition of such committees. Membership in the past, or the present, of a political party should automatically disqualify one, otherwise we would have a repetition of the shameful feature of the Fine Gael Coalition of 'jobs for the boys' which is now so widespread as to be obscene. Such committee members should be chosen for their patriotism, common sense and expert knowledge.

Whatever the answer is Haughey will have to face the fact that the present civil service system is just not satisfactory. The track record proves that beyond all doubt new and forceful methods will have to be tried, and woolly thinking put to one side. An example of such woolly thinking, for which the civil servants are not entirely responsible is the false idea that we do not have the money to pay our debts or invest in job creation.

We have plenty of money available but we are just not managing it properly. Savings on civil service squandermania, 'jobs for the boys', foreign junkets, consultants etc. could save us in excess of £1,000,000,000 every year. If we ceased being Britain's jailers and released our political prisoners, as De Valera did in 1932, ceased protecting the Border and put our army and gardaí to other uses we might well save up to £500,000,000 yearly.

I do not wish to criticise the entire civil service. We have had some excellent men and women among their ranks, a majority of whom never came before the public eye. But the evidence tends to show that decision-making is not their strong point. Running a country is not unlike running a successful business. Good, common sense management is what is required. Surely Haughey has sufficient experience of good management to tackle these problems successfully!

2.   The Course of Irish Justice

Over the past few years the affairs of the Department of Justice have appeared to the Irish people in such a bad light that public confidence in our system has taken what might be conservatively described as an unprecedented hammering. Various incidents of a grotesque, unprecedented, bizarre nature have highlighted this department as an almost perfect example of GUBU government. The Shercock case, the ill-treatment of prisoners, the re-emergence of the heavy gang, the seizure of private money, the Kerry babies, the extradition of Irishmen to a criminal regime, the anglicisation of the gardaí, the Spike Island fiasco, drugs in jails – the list is almost endless – have caused large sections of the Irish public to revise their thinking and to feel that Seán Doherty was an infinitely better and abler minister than the present incumbent. So disasterous have been the affairs of this department that it has inspired, in an unprecedented way, quite a number of books which focus a disturbing searchlight on some of the less laudable elements of its activities.

Its greatest failure, however, has been in relation to the Six Counties and quite a substantial section of the community now suspect that this deparment has allowed itself to be almost taken over by British thinking. Its assessment of the situation in the Six Counties is seriously at fault. In close line with this British thinking it sees that situation primarily as a security problem.

It does not see that the Nationalist people battered and brutalised for sixty years, only took to the gun when all reasonable political activity failed. It sees the Nationalists as terrorists and the British as goodies, when the reality is much more likely to be the other way around, and it is now actively co-operating in this British occupation. It seems to fully accept the new lie about the Six Counties being put out by the British to impress the USA and the EEC countries i.e. that their presence there is to save Europe from terrorism.

Again and again the reality of the situation has been put before them in books, newspapers and journals but they have chosen to ignore it. Writing in the *Sunday Press* in 1981 Desmond Fennell said:

> For serious people as distinct from actors nothing has changed in the North during the past ten days or the past ten years. The slaughter and suffering go on because the London and Dublin governments and their armed forces have not ended the injustice being done to the 600,000 Irish people in the Six Counties.
>
> It is the most basic injustice which can be done to any human community, their existence is not recognised by the political society in which they live. Their right to live as Irish people in their own country is denied by Britain and the Ulster British. An alien identity – British identity – is foisted on them by *force of arms* (italics mine). It is this injustice which has driven thousands of them, men and women, boys and girls, to take up arms against agents of British rule and to risk their lives and liberties recklessly. Their rebellion and the effort to suppress it, is the 'Northern Conflict'.

These harsh but true words seem to have passed over the heads of our Department of Justice – as have other and even harsher writings in books, newspapers and periodicals.

One of the most important of these recently published books has been *The Secret War* by Patsy McArdle, a Monaghan journalist who is a correspondent for various Irish and British newspapers, radio and television services. McArdle raises the whole question of cross-border co-operation and the seemingly double standards of the Coalition government, who condemn torture in the North on the one hand and collaborate with those carrying out the torture on the other. He raise some vital questions concerning the passing on of information by the gardaí to the North-

ern security forces, and the further passing on of such information to the Unionist terrorist organisation, the UVF, resulting
in the killing of young Irishmen by this organisation. On this
co-operation McArdle comments as follows:

> The main areas where cross-border security co-operation has
> improved is in communications, and the exchange of computerised
> information between the RUC and the garda síochána. The link
> up was extended to radio communications between mobile patrols
> across the border. . . Agreement reached had provided for gardaí,
> mainly members of the detective branch, to go northwards to make
> inquiries in specific cases and the same agreement stands of RUC
> men travelling southwards . . . RUC men have travelled sout!
> wards for conferences with senior garda officers on different
> occasions since 1980. . . While they (the British) depend to a great
> extent on information from the gardaí they have a separate feed-in
> through British army intelligence. Special liaison officers who work
> closely with the RUC provide collated information which is fed
> directly to intelligence officers at the various British army bases
> and this is readily available to the SAS.

The author draws attention to the unbelievable situation
where the Irish Department of Justice discriminates against Irish
Nationalists in favour of Unionists:

> In this political climate created by the government subversion and
> terrorism were equated with Republicanism, and the long list of
> Loyalist bombings and sectarian attacks in the South . . . was
> accepted with a sense of expectation. *Loyalist bombers, and indeed
> their British SAS cohorts, appeared to enjoy an unique immunity
> in their cross-border operations* (italics mine). Their organisational
> centres and supply routes to the South were never uncovered. An
> arms dump discovered at Redhills, Co. Cavan, was first believed
> to be an IRA cache but some months later it was admitted by
> Loyalists sources to be theirs.

The whole book raises some alarming questions: Why has our
Justice Department chosen to ignore fundamental human rights
violations in Border areas? Why are heavily armed SAS men,
if arrested, not treated as terrorists in the Dublin courts? Surely
this is illegal? How have photographs taken by the gardaí during
interrogation of alleged suspects ended up in the hands of the
security forces in the North? Why is the co-operation so one-

sided? Is the IRA the cause of the violence or are they only responding to British aggression and loyalist repression of the minority in the North?

To understand fully what this looks like to outsiders – who cannot really grasp it – we should set it into a European context. Can anyone imagine the West German government spying on its own citizens in East Germany struggling for re-unification, and informing and co-operating with the KGB, or allowing the East German secret police to cross the border at will on terrorist missions? Would Spain allow the British SAS to cross from Gibraltar into Spain to pursue and kill Spaniards who wanted the return of Spanish territory? How many thousands of collaborators were tried and executed after the Second World War for doing far less than our Department of Justice is doing today? It is when looked at in this light that the enormity of it strikes one. I doubt if there is any other nation that would do as we are doing and if many top Europeans see us as little more than a land of slaves and zombies we have only ourselves to blame.

One of the criticisms levelled at Haughey by Republicans is that for the brief periods he was in power he did not put a stop to this cross-border co-operation. That criticism has a solid basis and his failure to do so must be chalked up as a serious black mark against him. These were the days when he had a divided party and when he trusted Thatcher and the British but recently more than forty branches of Fianna Fáil have called for the withdrawal of the army and gardaí from the Border. There is now, within the party, a substantial groundswell towards its origin. Haughey quickly learned his lesson and, unlike FitzGerald, he learns fast. To trust the goodwill of the British again could easily destroy his career and split Fianna Fáil. He is unlikely to take that risk and I do not think it would be unreasonable to expect an end to gardaí-RUC co-operation, despite the yuppie cat-calls of helping 'terrorism' which he can safely ignore.

A second book which has opened the doors of truth to many Irish people is *Sheltering the Fugitive?* by the distinguished author Michael Farrell. This book concerns itself with one of the most disgraceful episodes in modern Irish history, the extradition of Irishmen to the occupied Six Counties.

Every civilised nation on earth, except Ireland, honours the basic right of all its citizens not to be extradited for political offences. Ireland recognised that right until the arrival of a Fine Gael Coalition under Garret FitzGerald. Even a previous Fine Gael Coalition recognised that right. The Taoiseach of that government, John A. Costello said:

> In order to prevent any further controversy or discussion on this point. . . there can be no question of our handing over either to the British or Six County authorities persons whom they may accuse of armed activities in Britain or the Six Counties.

This is a quite clear and unequivocal statement. (It is interesting to note that Costello refers to the 'Six Counties' while Garr FitzGerald adopts the preferred British title of 'Northern Ireland'.) But this view was to change. In an astonishing judgment the Chief Justice, T. F. O'Higgins, once a Fine Gael minister and son of one of the founders of the Irish fascist movement, the Blueshirts, said that to claim immunity from extradition one would have to show that the political actions were 'what reasonable civilised people would regard as political activity'. He did not exactly define that phrase and this judgment has given rise to many questions. I know scores of 'reasonable civilised people' including judges, who would reject Mr O'Higgins' concept out of hand, as both legally unsound and indeed dangerous.

When Mr O'Higgins was appointed to the job of a judge in the European Court he was replaced in the Supreme Court by Mr Justice Finlay. The legal world were now more than curious to see if Justice Finlay would follow the same extraordinary line as Justice O'Higgins. This curiosity was given a special edge by a statement made by Justice Finlay in 1974 in the Burns case when he said:

> . . . it seems to me that the safe-keeping of explosives for an organisation attempting to overthrow the state by violence is according to that test an   offence of a *political nature* (italics mine).

He accordingly refused to extradite Fr Burns.

By 1984 that judgment seems to have slipped his memory. In the Quinn case he said:

> This court cannot, it seems to me, interpret an Act of the Oireachtas as having the intention to grant immunity from extradition to a

person charged with an offence, the admitted purpose of which is to further or facilitate the overthrow by violence of the Constitution and of the organs of the State established thereby.

Quinn was accordingly extradited. Michael Farrell comments:

If the court sticks to this line and applies it to the IRA as well as the INLA – as logically it must – extradition will become automatic for members of Republican paramilitary groups. Successive governments – most notably Liam Cosgrave's at the time of the Sunningdale conference – will have been wrong about extradition and so will the Irish delegation on the 1974 Law Enforcement Commission. . .

Such a total reversal of policy amounts effectively to changing the law, and changing it on the basis of a controversial and distinctly arguable interpretation of the objects of the IRA and the INLA. Such a decision would seem to be the prerogative of the Oireachtas rather than the courts. . .

In the common view as well it looked distinctly as if the Supreme Court had decided by 1982 that members of the IRA or INLA accused of crimes in the North or Britain should be extradited and had since been casting about for arguments to justify its action.

This last paragraph highlights the nub of the matter, namely *public confidence in our courts*. I do not for one moment wish to suggest that any of the judges in question acted other than in accordance with their legal lights. But if one looks at various chains of events one cannot help detecting a growing suspicion in the mind of the public that political considerations have an undue bearing on judicial decisions. The anti-Republican paranoia of the present Fine Gael Coalition has permeated many aspects of the state machinery. The question now being asked by an increasing number of responsible people is: *Has this paranoia now invaded the courts?* I am not suggesting it has but what I am saying is that there are many raised eyebrows at some recent events. To prevent these misgivings spreading to the point where a major breakdown in public confidence in the law would occur Mr Haughey will have to act quickly, ruthlessly and decisively. The likelihood is that he will do so.

In a number of comments made after these Supreme Court decisions he made it quite clear that the extradition of Irish citizens to Northern Ireland must not be allowed to continue.

He disagreed with the court's decision and correctly stated that the entire system of the administration of justice in the North has been totally discredited and that no court should hand over any of our citizens. He has also publicly opposed the ratification of a US-British treaty to extradite Irishmen for political offences. This would seem to indicate that he is committed to amending the law so as to ensure for all time courts cannot ever extradite an Irishman to the Six Counties.

A very good example of the somewhat shameful level to which both our gardaí and our Minister for Justice, Michael Noonan have reached is well illustrated by an incident which took place in April 1985. One of the garda organisations held its annual conference in Bundoran and to that conference they invited a representative of the Northern Ireland Police Federation, who was given two standing ovations. While I am not criticising in any way the particular individual who attended, it is certainly strange that Irish gardaí should so honour a police force found guilty by an international court of inhuman treatment of prisoners, who pursue a 'shoot-to-kill' policy against innocent people and who have bribed informers and perjurers to give evidence against Irish citizens. In his speech of welcome Mr Noonan is reported as having said that he particularly welcomed the representative from the North who had suffered so much in their efforts to restore peace and law and order in that part of the country. Mr Noonan must have forgotten his own Taoiseach's condemnation of that force, as he must have overlooked all the published material which has so thoroughly discredited the police in the Six Counties. The mind boggles at such thinking by an Irish Minister for Justice.

This whole attitude of the gardaí, and indeed the Minister, is a far cry from the noble sentiments expressed by Haughey when he spoke at the opening of the Garda Training Centre at Templemore in Co. Tipperary.

> To those of us who have read Davis, Sheehan and Kickham it is difficult not to succumb to the belief that Tipperary is, indeed, the very heart of Ireland. I know of no county in which the atmosphere would be more suitable for the training of our young gardaí, or where they would be more likely to become imbued with a patriotic

outlook and a regard for all that is valuable and precious in Irish life.

But then Bundoran is a long, long way from Tipperary – and Mr Noonan a far, far cry from Davis or Kickham.

Reforming this department which has deteriorated so much under the present minister, Mr Noonan, described by one elected colleague in Dáil Éireann as 'the most worthless and useless member of the cabinet ever to come from Limerick', will be no easy task. The suspicion that exists in the minds of large sections of the Irish people is that this department has allowed itself to come dangerously close to becoming a mere echo of the British Home Office. Again the reforms here will have to be drastic and far-reaching.

3. The Servile Service
Millions of pounds of your money and mine is being spent every year on a service whose principal function it is to represent and promote the point of view of the Irish people in foreign countries. This expenditure would indeed be well worth while if it did just that. Unfortunately its performance falls far short of that ideal. Under a confused Fianna Fáil and a co-operative Fine Gael this costly service slowly and gradually moved into the British orbit and became, not the voice of the Irish people, but a kind of subordinate back-up service supporting the British view of Ireland in foreign countries. Like the foreign service of Iron Curtain countries, who must look over their shoulders to see what the Russians are thinking, our Irish foreign service must also look over its shoulder and take its cue from the British viewpoint. This is a far cry from the days of De Valera when each Irish embassy was a centre of political and cultural activity and somewhat of a thorn in the side of the British in almost every country. In those days our embassies were not ashamed to tell the world that Ireland was a country of Thirty-Two counties, Six of which were forcibly occupied by the British. Now they are so under the influence of the British that one rarely, if ever, hears them making this claim. Rather, when some do timidly speak out they enunciate most respectfully that which they hope will meet with the approval of the British ambassadors. Even in those countries where they have slightly exerted themselves, their political insensitivity has caused them to take steps which have done the

Irish nation a great deal more harm than good.

The United States is one such country. It is an illusion to think that American political leaders have any special goodwill towards Ireland. For the most part, they are hard-headed politicians motivated by greed and if they appear to make noises sympathetic to Ireland it is with a view to capturing the massive Irish vote in the United States. It is this political greed that the Irish foreign service has failed to comprehend, understand and exploit.

This bad error of judgment is why we have thrown in our lot with a group known as the Friends of Ireland, headed by Senator Tip O'Neill, a well-meaning, if uninformed, politician, and a light-weight politician Senator Moynihan, recently described as 'England's best friend in Congress'. These men are first and foremost Americans who will always put the interests of the United States first and in a global sense the interests of the United States *are the interests of Britain*. They would like to see a peaceful solution in the Six Counties if for no other reason than that it would suit American foreign policy to have a trouble-free zone there, so that NATO could build its bases in peace, but it is an illusion to think that they will put the interests of Ireland before those of Britain. A recent speech by O'Neill would lead one to suspect that he believes the Irish to be a lot of zombies unable to think for themselves or unable to see through his verbiage. In this speech he said that guns would solve nothing and only constitutional politics would work. That kind of nonsense presumes he never heard of El Salvador, Nicaragua, Granada, Afganistan or the Falklands.

Moynihan seems to be very poorly informed on the Six Counties. Perhaps if he travelled there incognito and as a Catholic tried to get a job he might learn at first hand the realities of being an out-of-work Catholic in the Six Counties. His ignorance recently led him to insult Ireland's greatest living Irishman, Nobel Peace prize-winner Seán MacBride, when Mr MacBride was drawing public attention to discrimination practised against Nationalists in the Six Counties and suggesting a set of principles ensuring fair treatment for all. Moynihan attacked these principles as a 'sinister campaign to cause economic havoc in Northern Ireland by causing American disinvestment and thereby helping

Northern "terrorists".' Any child on the street could have told Moynihan that widespread discrimination is at present practised against Catholics and Nationalists in almost very branch of industry and the civil service. Mr MacBride was merely trying to lay down some guidelines for American firms to ensure fair play.

Fine Gael have thrown their lot in with this group who despite the grand sounding title of their organisation, and the fact that some are genuinely interested in Ireland, are not by any stretch of imagination real friends of Ireland and a majority might be more accurately described as friends of England. They are first and foremost American politicians and when the chips are down their real interest in Ireland is peripheral. Yet our foreign office somewhat stupidly still believes that help will come from them and that they really represent Irish-American opinion. Nothing could be further from the truth and it is this erroneous political assessment by our government and civil service that is disquieting.

If our foreign service had an intelligent perceptive insight into Irish-American affairs they would long ago have realised that the Irish National Caucus, the AOH, the Ad Hoc Committee and indeed Noraid itself are far more representative of Irish opinion and are far more likely to influence United States opinion on the realities of the occupation of the Six Counties.

Again and again Charles Haughey has pointed out how we have failed to use this powerful force in the USA to help solve the Northern problem. Our foreign office, perhaps under the influence of Fine Gael, still clings to the O'Neills and Moynihans whose track record so far is that they have achieved practically *nothing* for Ireland and who in the long run will stand first and foremost for America, which means for England in the global sense. That is the *realpolitik* of the situation, and no high sounding speeches can alter that fact.

In a recent newspaper article Tim Pat Coogan put it succinctly:

> We should be harnessing American opinion as a potentially powerful agent for change on British thinking and we should cut out a lot of our nonsensical foreign affairs government interpretation of how to influence the vital ingredient of Irish-American public opinion in this.

Unfortunately we are by no means harnessing Irish American

opinion to the full. Our foreign service does not seem to have grasped, in the same way as the Jews did, the very simple political fact that the United States government will do nothing for Ireland unless we force them to do so by threatening them with the massive Irish vote in the United States – now estimated at 40,000,000.

When the Jewish state of Israel was being established the Jews pressurised Truman into giving them what they wanted by threatening him with the loss of the American-Jewish vote, which was less than 1,000,000. Truman gave in. His actual comment was: 'I have to answer to hundreds of thousands of Jews. I do not have hundreds of thousands of Arabs among my constituents.' This alarming admission is real hard core politics which we Irish should have long ago grasped. The Jews brought the same pressure to bear on successive United States presidents, always with a high degree of success, while we have hopelessly failed to make any impact.

We have a far greater voting clout in America than the Jews but our foreign service does not seem to have either the political cop-on to recognise it or the resolution to do anything about it. Instead we have been diplomatically hoodwinked and the political clout fragmented. We have thrown in our lot with the wrong people and poured abuse on great Irishmen like Michael Flannery and great friends of Ireland like Mario Baggio and Martin Galvin and their organisations. Only recently Mr Peter Barry insulted one of the most powerful Irish-American groups by telling them to go home when they visited Ireland – much to the delight of the British who want to prevent at all costs any unity of Irish forces in America. Again and again Haughey has referred to this powerful force and appealed for unity of action, but nothing happened because our foreign service was gazing in the opposite direction – across the Irish sea.

It is, however, only fair to point out that any Fine Gael dominated government will get very little Irish-American support. The Irish in America had to leave their homeland largely because of generations of British brutality and savagery and their children have long memories. As well, the most influential members of many Irish-American organisations today are either themselves, or their parents were, victims of more brutalities perpetrated immediately after the Civil War, particularly by the

CID attached to the infamous Oriel House. They too have long memories and when the successors of that regime come with their repertoire of alien-inspired platitudes they are unlikely to get much of a hearing.

But I cannot over-emphasïse the importance of harnessing the Irish-American vote. It was that all-important vote which helped to force the British to the negotiation table in 1921, and it can still do so in 1986 or 1987 if it is intelligently harnessed.

Fine Gael's poor grasp of the realities of the American scene was given voice when FitzGerald wanted Haughey to condemn some Irish-American organisations because they were sympathetic to the IRA. Haughey replied:

> What is required is not mere condemnation but effective action to provide those who are in sympathy with the objectives of Irish unity with an alternative – a clear objective and a policy which Irish-Americans can support.

The over-riding principle here is that American presidents and American governments have no interest in Ireland except to capture the Irish vote. They have no interest in the Six Counties except that it can be used for NATO bases and when they offer vast sums in financial aid to the Six Counties it is purely for selfish reasons. How does one drum that simple truth into the heads of our foreign service?

If we look at the operation of our foreign service in other countries we will be equally disappointed. In Britain itself we surely must be able to influence close on 1,000,000 votes. We have a vast Irish population there capable of influencing an election vote but again have made no effective use of this immense power.

I am quite amazed at the fact that an important poll reported in the *Troops Out Bulletin* never got adequate coverage in the Irish media. According to this report:

> Fifty-eight per cent of the people in Britain are in favour of a united Ireland. A poll conducted in 1984 has been published by Jowell and Airey under the title 'British Social Attitudes'. The poll also shows that fifty-nine per cent think that British troops should be withdrawn from the North of Ireland.

Is it not quite extraordinary that this poll got so little coverage in the Irish media? If the poll showed the opposite result could we expect the same stony silence?

Neverthelesss if 58% of the British people want a United Ireland surely this is an excellent basis for our foreign service to work on. But like the rabbit and the snake we seem to be paralysed by British arrogance.

Perhaps that which illustrates best our ineptitude in Britain is the way in which our foreign service has reacted to the Prevention of Terrorism Act (the PTA). This act was passed in England in 1974 as a very temporary measure designed to protect people's safety but like so many other pieces of British legislation it has now become an act of unprecedented terror for all Irish people living in Britain as well as those travelling to and fro. Des Hickey writing in the *Sunday Independent* commented:

> So far as the Irish population is concerned all are now guilty until proven innocent. The harassment of the Irish in recent months under the Prevention of Terrorism Act is approaching the harassment of the Jewish population in Germany in the Thirties.

This analogy with Nazi Germany is by no means exaggerated. More than 6,000 Irish people have been taken into custody, held for seven days and refused the basic rights to inform their relatives or contact a solicitor. Old men and old women as well as the young have been beaten, tortured, stripped naked, left in cells with neon lighting resulting in complete disorientation. Many of the techniques of interrogation used by the Gestapo are now being used by the British special branch against the Irish. 'Racism in the British police force is now directed more against the Irish than the West Indians,' Patrica Hewett, General Secretary of the Camden Town National Council for Civil Liberties is reported to have said. 'The police harass, arrest and interrogate Irish people who are usually innocent. In one case they lifted a household of twenty-three people. There have also been cases where children have actually been arrested.' In a very revealing article in the *Sunday World* Tony Bradley reported from London quoting various witnesses:

> They'll pull somebody in and tell him or her that if they don't co-operate the word will be spread in the Irish community that

they're a male homosexual or a lesbian. . . They go to an Irishman's employer asking for the man and just mentioning they are from Scotland Yard Bomb Squad.

This often results in a man losing his job. Again according to one of Mr Bradley's informants they pick up Irishmen on their way to take up a job on the Continent, travelling via London, and deport them back to Ireland. In this way the men will lose their jobs.

One result of this is that many Irish people travelling to the Continent will not travel through England. I am one of these people. I have been tipped off that if I go to England I should be prepared for an extended stay. According to my informant I am a thorn in their sides because of my various writings. That indeed is a compliment! I could get six or seven years for failing to provide information, as some unfortunate innocent Irishmen now know to their cost, or indeed they would have no scruple in planting a gun or explosive in my luggage and everyone knows the kind of justice I could expect from British courts. How many other writers are in the same position? If we were to treat British visitors proportionately in the same way as they treat us we would need to arrest and hold 100,000 persons each year. Perhaps we should consider doing so if for nothing else but to teach them a lesson.

But there is one really sinister element in all this and that is that most of the information upon which they base their interrogation is *supplied to them by the Irish gardaí*. Surely this is outrageous. But perhaps it explains why our foreign service is inactive here. How could our Department of Foreign Affairs protest effectively if our Department of Justice is supplying the information upon which arrests and interrogations are being carried out. For indeed our Department of Foreign Affairs are doing virtually nothing effective. Des Hickey in the *Sunday Independent* comments:

> Must our department of Foreigh Affairs turn a bland face and a blind eye to this harassment? Surely there is some way that innocent Irish people can be protected from increasing racial harassment?

Mr Tony Gregory TD contacted the Department of Foreign Affairs to enquire about the arrest of one of his constituents and found them to be completely disinterested.

Referring to one case, that of Mr James McCormack, the *Irish Press* editorialised:

> In the case of Mr McCormack, not only did the British police act in a disgraceful manner to humiliate and embarrass an Irish citizen but members of the garda síochána, for reasons known only to themselves, seem to have assisted in that operation with gusto. . .
>
> One can be very sure that if British visitors were treated in this country to the sort of harassment which the Irish have had to endure at British ports the British ambassador would be a constant visitor to Iveagh House.

But the Irish foreign service has sung dumb and it has been left to honourable English voices to help the defenceless Irish. Mrs Harriet Harman, Labour MP for Peckham, referring to the abuse of this act said:

> I want to know why this act with its exceptional powers was used against two men whom the police acknowledge have no connection with terrorism.

Mr Michael Flannery, MP for Sheffield, also joined in the protest and called for an inquiry into what he described as 'this deplorable affair'.

The Irish in Britian organised themselves into a representation group and made formal representation to the Irish government through the Irish embassy to condemn the Prevention of Terrorism Act and to monitor each case in which it was used against the Irish community. Both the embassy in London and the Department of Foreign affairs refused the requests. Through their press officer the Irish Representation group said:

> We find it totally unacceptable for the Irish people to be left without proper consular facilities when their civil rights are threatened.

This almost incredible attitude of our foreign service surely should be changed.

What about Europe? Unfortunately the case here is much the same. Lecturers presenting the British point of view speak at important centres, such as universities, colleges and seminars give a totally distorted point of view on Northern Ireland. There seems to be a regular panel of such lecturers to ensure that at least once a year the British viewpoint, however false, is put before the university and higher education groups. Officials of the various British embassies maintain regular contact with all branches of the media, and as in Ireland, lavishly entertain journalists and writers to ensure that only British propaganda gets through. All this is done virtually without a whimper from the Irish embassies. It seems as if they are paralysed with fear of offending the British.

In his clear-headed and perceptive book *An End to Silence* Des Wilson says:

> A very large amount of money is spent by the British government on propaganda. . . The printed propaganda shows a strange mixture of sophistication and naïvety. The standard of production of information sheets etc. which flood the American universities, church magazines and newspapers is high; the quality of argument is low. . . In recent years they have had to exert themselves more as the case for British withdrawal from Ireland has been seen to be both democratic and rational. . . If it had not been for the ready co-operation of successive Irish governments British propaganda would probably have been a more difficult task. . . every time a major political event occurred in Ireland the British representative in the Vatican went to the Vatican Secretariate of State . . . to give the official British version.

The only organisation which effectively puts the Irish point of view on the Continent are Sinn Féin. They regularly attend the British lectures and question the lecturers, much to their embarrassment. In a number of cities on the Continent Sinn Féin also maintain offices and publish leaflets and pamphlets in the language of the country, counteracting the British falsehoods. This is slowly proving effective with the continental media who have now been made wary and suspicious of British news. They now tend to send their own representatives to the Six Counties from time to time and get first hand information for themselves.

But these small successes reflect no glory on our own foreign service who are strangely silent in the face of all the falsehoods being circulated by the British. I do not wish to put the entire blame on the officials of our foreign service. They have to take orders from the government and if a nation has a government such as our present Coalition one cannot expect courage and resolution from such a source.

Let me give an example of the helpless grasp our present Minister for Foreign Affairs has of world affairs. Over the next few years Britain will return the colony of Hong Kong to China. (It is intriguing to speculate if they would hand it over if China were a small weak nation like Ireland.) When this was announced the Spanish government sent its foreign minister to Peking where he stated publicly that China and Spain have a common interest in having occupied territories returned. In this way he drew international attention once again to the British occupation of Gibraltar and got world-wide publicity. Here was a glorious opportunity for our foreign minister to visit China also and draw attention to the analogy between the Six Counties and Hong Kong and in this way generate world wide publicity. Unfortunately the significance of all this passed over the minister's head.

Again in August 1985 when the security forces in Northern Ireland were operating a 'shoot-to-kill' policy; when the United States was trying to change the extradition laws; when the British army was crossing our Border and harassing Irish citizens at least once a week and when Irish prisoners were being tortured in British jails; the main thrust and occupation of the Irish foreign service was with the harmless activities of a New York pipe band in Bundoran! That almost beats the classic case of the League of Nations who were engrossed in discussions concerning changes in traffic lights the day the Second World War broke out!

Nevertheless our civil servants could, if they wanted to, make it difficult for a government to pursue such a subservient course by opposing these policies in every legal way open to them. But while there are some officials of the highest calibre and integrity within their ranks, others, with an eye on jobs and promotion, may take their cue from the reigning government.

Once again Haughey will face a formidable task in reforming this service. To start with, the appointment of a first class minister would seem obvious. I mention this because in the past this office was entrusted to men who were unable for the job – some in fact mere nonentities – who delegated far too much to the civil service with such sad consequences for the nation.

New men may well be needed for a fresh vigorous onslaught on the spread of British falsehoods abroad, particularly to refute the lie that Britain is fighting 'terrorism' in the North. All this will again require a strong degree of ruthlessness on Haughey's part, a ruthlessness that will not be deflected by the advice or threats of phoney friends. Here again he will be required to lift this service out of its servility, to make it proud of its Irishness, and above all to make Irish people abroad proud of their embassies and not ashamed.

I have dealt at length with these few state institutions but it would be possible to write at length on the other departments of state. All seem to be paralysed by the servile mind which emanates from the very top. Again I repeat: only the elimination of this servile mind can save us. Not so long ago a great Irish priest remarked:

> There is a famine abroad – a famine not of bread nor of gold, but a famine of great men. We are stained with mediocrity, we are dying of ordinariness, we are perishing of pettiness.

How long more are we required to tolerate and pay for this?

5: The Iron Hand in the Velvet Glove

I believe that a Labour Party that went into an election committed to a speedy withdrawal from Ireland would receive massive popular support because we speak for the majority of men and women in this country when we speak for Britain getting out of Ireland
– KEN LIVINGSTONE, Chairman, Greater London Council.

I am as anxious as anyone for the material prosperity of Ireland and the Irish people but I cannot do anything that would make the people hang their heads. The Irish would not want me to save them materially at the expense of their national honour
– EAMON DE VALERA

Our object in building up the country economically must not be lost sight of. The object is not to be able to boast of enormous wealth or of a great volume of trade for their own sake. . . It is not to show a great national balance sheet, not to point to a people producing wealth, not the self-obliteration of a hive of bees. The real riches of the Irish nation will be the men and women of the Irish nation, the extent to which they are rich in body and mind and character.
– MICHAEL COLLINS

When I feed the hungry they call me a saint. When I ask why there is hunger they call me a communist.
– DOM HELDER CAMERA.

I have tried in the previous chapters to draw attention to a few – but only a few – of the principal areas where immediate corrective action is required – statesmanlike action – if Ireland is to become a real nation once again. I have not touched upon the frightening economic situation where we are hurtling towards disaster, in a country where it is more profitable to take the dole than to work, where no investor with an ounce of common sense would be attracted by Irish industry, where most businesses or enterprises are so crippled by taxation that instead of trying to expand, create wealth and employment, they are struggling to merely survive. Of this stagnant state, where our only thriving industry seems to be the prison industry, I have not written since it would take many volumes to cover it, even superficially. As well, I have said again and again our problems are *not* basically economic. They are problems of national morale and national backbone. The words of William Martin Murphy written so many years ago are valid today: 'Carson got all he wanted by guts and backbone. Our men possess neither one nor the other.'

Neither have I touched on our membership of the EEC where the reality bears little resemblence to the packet we were sold. The harsh facts are that since we joined the EEC virtually all our traditional industries have closed down, unemployment has soared, our farmers are nearly bankrupt, personal taxation is at a crippling level and arising from all these factors we have a major breakdown in law and order. Countries such as Austria, Sweden, Switzerland, Norway and Finland, who did not join the EEC, reduced unemployment to 3½% while we increased ours to 18%. Yet in spite of these facts staring us in the face Mr Peter Barry told us in January 1985 that Fine Gael stood 100% behind continued membership. It is hard to credit this unbelievable political judgment. To examine this in detail and to show how an intelligent government in Greenland handled a similar problem would again require a book in itself. Here, once more, I emphasise my main theme, that if we had a national morale and an unqualified patriotism we would find a quick solution.

Neither have I touched on the unbelievable shame of our radio and television services, where alone among the countries of the world these services are so often used to decry every noble national sentiment and to promote the views of the British who are so delighted with our media subservience.

All in all there are many major omissions in this book but I do not see this as a great defect. The basic principle underlying what I have written here is that *if the national morale is strong and vibrant everything else follows and fits into place* provided we have a statesman to lead us.

Allied closely to national morale is national leadership of the calibre of Collins, De Valera, De Gaulle, Adenauer and Lincoln. As these lines are being written (summer 1985) our national leadership, as constituted in the Fine Gael-Labour Coalition, is surely recognised by most Irish people as having reached the lowest level since the battle of Kinsale. The broken, battered, suppressed nation that Ireland was during the penal days had better leadership and better morale than today. Our present-day rulers do not seem to be aware of even the most rudimentary qualities needed for good leadership and wise statesmanship.

Intelligence is an obvious quality needed in any statesman but that which is known as political intelligence is even more important. From political intelligence stems political *sensitivity* which enables a leader to sense and estimate with reasonable accuracy the thoughts and feelings of the public. De Valera, despite many other failings, was a master in this theatre of operations. He could read the mind of the Irish people with amazing accuracy. Throughout his long political career he correctly sensed that deep down in the hearts of the Irish there was a hard core of *patriotism and Republicanism*. Again and again he appealed to these emotions and because of this enjoyed success after success until late in life when he became so embedded in the establishment that he lost his grip.

There is every reason to believe that Mr Haughey has that incisive political sensitivity which enables him to judge the inner patriotic spirit of the Irish people. It is unlikely that in the future he will ever ally himself with the British viewpoint against Republicanism. This has been the cardinal political error of Fine Gael and explains why they have never been able to get an over-all majority or form a government on their own. They are simply seen by too many people as weak in the face of the British.

As I have said earlier Haughey shares with great statesmen past and present the proven ability to learn *from his own mistakes*. It is more than likely that he has long recognised the fundamental error of trusting any British politician. He must now know that the only language the British understand is the language of obdurate and intransigent toughness, and if he still has any doubts about that a glance at the recent history of Israel should remove any uncertainty from his mind.

In a small emerging country like ours any statesman worth his salt must know what he wants for the country – in other words he must have *vision*. Now vision can have many different shades of meaning not all of which are worthy of a statesman. No one, for example, can deny that Garret FitzGerald has vision but it is a kind of silly vision which sees everything upside down, a vision which can only remind one of a knight wildly galloping in the wrong direction with his armour on back to front.

The vision of an Irish leader today ought to be based on the vision of Pearse who gave expression to it in the 1916 proclamation. De Gaulle found his inspiration for a new France in the person of Joan of Arc despite the yelps of the yuppies of his day which he rightly ignored. De Valera's vision of Ireland in 1943 is now being sneered at by some, yet they never ask themselves the question – is that which replaced it – murder, robberies, muggings, bulging jails, drugs, unemployment – the better ideal?

Haughey seems to have a clearer vision of the Ireland he wants – a good blend of idealism and realism. Speaking at the Irish Club in London he said:

> In Ireland today we believe as passionately as ever in the concept of a United Ireland, that it is in the natural order of things and that some day it will come about. In the meantime however we do not intend to sulk in our tents. We intend to get on with the job of building up our country and playing our part as good citizens of the world. We are working and planning to build up our industry, develop our agriculture, distribute our national income in accordance with the principles of social justice, provide our people with a full and comprehensive system of education and so create a society which all Irishmen will come to look upon with pride and wish to participate in.

Here we have a statesmanlike vision that is not ashamed to put a united Ireland first. There is no grovelling to the prejudice of fanatics or to the arrogance of the invaders. While endeavouring to achieve that, the material prosperity of the people can also be achieved. Elsewhere he said:

> We must seek to create. . . communities which are as integrated as possible and where a real community feeling prevails and is seen by all to prevail, where everyone is conscious of belonging, where there are no tensions caused by barriers of class or religion.

For Haughey the vision of Pearse is not a mere catch-cry. It is a reality. Speaking to farmers he said:

> Doing something for the future of one's country is a sure sign of life. Earlier generations of Irish farmers made few improvements because, being tenants at will, they had no purpose for doing so.

1916 changed this. The present and each future generation owe it
to the men of 1916 to make well organised and intelligent efforts
to improve the land of Ireland and exploit its resources. . . The
soil is our greatest raw material and Pearse asserted the right of
the Irish people to hold and control the land.

But important and all as vision is, it alone does not make for
good leadership. To realise the vision calls for decisiveness in
order to bring that vision to fruition. Ireland is full of those who
dream the most exciting dreams for the future of our country
but on the ground there are very few who have the strength or
resolution to make these dreams a reality.

Haughey's ministerial career would seem to indicate that lack
of decisiveness is not one of his faults. As Minister for Justice
his programme of law reform was decisive and imaginative. Peter
Berry, the Secretary of the Department of Justice, who was
certainly no friend of Haughey's said that of the fourteen ministers he worked under Haughey was the ablest. Berry described
him as 'dynamic and a joy to work with'. So brilliant was
Haughey's law reform programme that it served as a model for
many other emerging nations engaged in removing the shackles
of colonialism.

As Minister for Agriculture he saw clearly that farming was
our fundamental industry and he set about improving the lot of
farmers and creating a climate in which this industry could reach
its optimum. In this context he said:

> It is easy to go around telling farmers that they are ignored and
> neglected. . . It is not so easy to preach the obvious truth that the
> only sure and lasting way for the farmer to better his position and
> that of his family is to get more from his holding, to improve his
> production and his efficiency and that the government are provid-
> ing assistance in almost every conceivable way to help him to do
> this. . . We have a comprehensive structure of schemes and ser-
> vices at the disposal of the farmer to help him to get ahead but
> there is always room for discussion about them. . . We must not
> listen only to the economist and the bureaucratic planner who
> think of agriculture as simply another section of the economy.

In Haughey's brief period in this ministry there was no short-
age of decisiveness in those various schemes promulgated to put
the industry on a durable and well-founded footing.

As the youngest Finance Minister in Europe he brought in free transport for the old, giving relief and happiness to senior citizens in their declining years. Only the old themselves realise what a boon that is. His legislation on tax exemption for writers and artists was one of the most imaginative ever enacted in any country. Today its operation has sadly been thwarted by the civil service and has become virtually ineffective. His budgets were models of what a budget should be. He realised that unless the spirit of enterprise was encouraged and developed there could be only stagnation. And this spirit of enterprise depended to a considerable degree on the ability of entrepreneurs to make profits. He said once:

> I should like to put forward the proposition that the trouble with this country is that too many people are making insufficient profits. Too many people are making losses. . . It would be well for this country from every point of view, and particularly from the point of view of the weaker sections of the community if our industrialists were put in a position where they could make adequate profits which would ensure their continuation in business and their being able to finance further expansion.

The wisdom of this statement contasts starkly with the muddled financial thinking being imposed upon us in the Ireland of today, where in order to try to placate Labour support, the making of profit is made to look like a crime with the result that factory after factory is closing down and men and women who gave a lifetime of service are now facing an old age of penury. Haughey is quite clear and decisive on the function of government:

> A good government is on top of the situation, ahead of events. They should never allow economic difficulties to progress to the point where they no longer have the freedom to follow their own policies for the betterment of the community but are rather forced by the exigencies of the situation to adopt one expedient after another. . . We believe that the government must direct and guide the economy in the way they want it to go.

One of the major decisions made by Haughey which required a great deal of moral courage was his taking on the tobacco companies, and imposing severe restrictions on tobacco sponsorship because he was satisfied that smoking was a major evil. These companies were very wealthy and powerful but once he was convinced of the damage their products were causing, he not only put curbs on them but gave up smoking himself.

One of the criticisms made against Haughey is that, despite his brilliant record as a minister, during his first period as Taoiseach he showed himself to be seriously indecisive. It was alleged that he did absolutely nothing and let things drift – that he did not know what to do with power when he got it.

Now I am always intrigued by the fact that whenever anything bad can be said about Haughey it will be said loudly and openly, without any attempt being made to examine in depth the prevailing circumstances. Such one-sided treatment is not, however, meted out to others. No matter how many major blunders they make certain elements in the media will always either find or invent excuses for them.

It may well be that Haughey was indecisive during that period but surely the public were entitled to be told by the media the cirmcumstances so that they could make up their own minds.

When he was elected Taoiseach it is generally known that only one minister had voted for him. The others opposed him, some particularly viciously – so the first thing he inherited was a cabinet of opponents. How many of us would like to have to work with a board who opposed us. Although such a situation does not encourage great decisiveness, many now believe he should have struck them hard and unmercifully. If the situation were a business one and not political, a good managing director on taking over control would have sacked most of them. But in politics this might have led to a major split in the party and Haughey could not risk that. So he was stuck with them and indeed with a lot of others in the party who were opposed to him. His chief rival in the party, George Colley, proved himself too peevish to accept the democratic vote of the majority in spite of the many olive branches offered by Haughey and instead of throwing his weight behind the party and the leader he actually conducted a secret campaign against Haughey's authority – something totally opposed to the great traditions of Fianna Fáil. The fact that this campaign was even tolerated shows the depth to which Fianna Fáil as an organisation had sunk.

Kevin Boland in *The Rise and Decline of Fianna Fáil* describes the Fianna Fáil party at the time in the harshest of words:

> A once proud, idealistic and disciplined party has degenerated into
> a miserable, unprincipled and leaderless rabble, a party that
> demonstrates its own chronic instability with every political wind
> that blows, incongruously pleading to be allowed to provide stable
> government, while the leader leads in the knowledge that he is
> surrounded by colleagues ready to pounce if he makes one false
> step.

Now it may be that Haughey was indecisive in that period but
with such a dreadful unsavoury mess all around him there might
well be extenuating circumstances. It was the right of the public
to have those circumstances pointed out to them, but instead,
the bulk of the media sang dumb and only raised their voices
when there was opportunity to attack Haughey.

Allied to the quality of decisiveness is the all important quality
of ruthlessness. In this sphere Haughey can be justly faulted. I
have dealt with this to some extent in *Operation Brogue*:

> He (Haughey) is indeed too tolerant, too modest and too temperate
> with those who would destroy him at the drop of a hat. In running
> a party like Fianna Fáil, which has within it elements more at home
> with Fine Gael, there is no room for kind-heartedness. A political
> party, like an army, is held together by iron discipline. One chink
> in the armour and it widens and spreads and ultimately bursts
> asunder. . .
>
> I emphasise very much the extreme dangers of being too nice
> or too soft. Elsewhere I have criticised Haughey severely for his
> softness with Thatcher during the hunger-strike. Had he hit her
> right between the eyes by sending home the British ambassador,
> closing the Border, ending all co-operation the chances are she
> would have yielded. It is the only kind of language she understands.
> Had he done so at the time he would have won the election with
> an over-all majority, the trauma of the following years would not
> have happened, and we would not be today in the sad position of
> being little more than Britain's puppet. Did Thatcher foresee this?
> Did she know by her intransigence Haughey would be defeated
> and she could be sure of a government more pliable to her
> demands? Look at the end result. Who gained as a result of his
> lack of ruthlessness?

Ruthlessness is a quality that all great world statesmen had and used with effect. In the Irish milieu ruthlessness is one of the most important qualities any Irish statesman can have *when dealing with the British*. De Valera had it in his early days in charge of the state but in his later days, particularly as president he succumbed to the British point of view. Lemass had it but in his later years he too seemed to move closer to the British point of view. Both of these men started off by treating the British with great ruthlessness and ended their lives much more closely aligned to the British, while the British had not moved one inch. It is intriguing that the opposite seems to have happened in Haughey's case. He started off with a tactful conciliatory approach towards the British. It was quickly intimated to him who was the overseer and he was given the contemptuous slap in the face especially reserved for the Irish. Unlike FitzGerald, however, who grovelled and came back for more, Haughey reacted and hit back over the Falklands issue. This infuriated the British, and his courageous attitude here was the spark that started off the campaign of vilification against him. It was important to the British that they keep Irish politicians in their place, obedient and subservient. Haughey failed them in this and punishment therefore had to be meted out to him, as a warning to other Irish politicians to remember their proper station in life and not go against their 'betters'.

Here an important point often overlooked is that he *has* the capacity for ruthlessness and can use it too. He surely will have to use it much more in the future.

One area where this ruthlessness will be called for is in relationship with Britain concerning the Six Counties. This may well call for some form of recognition of the role of the IRA in the North. I know this is a radical suggestion and I may be severely criticised for it. Nevertheless, judged by world standards, the IRA are freedom-fighters and not terrorists. In an important article in *The Readers Digest* called *Standing Up For Freedom Fighters*, US Secretary of State, George Schultz said *inter alia*:

> . . . for a revolution is sweeping the world today – a democratic revolution which is capturing the imagination and passions of the brave men and women on every continent. They seek indepen-

dence, freedom and human rights. . .

In each situation it must always be clear on whose side we are on – the side of those who want to see a world based on respect for national independence, for human rights, for freedom and the rule of law. Wherever possible, the path to that world should be through peaceful, political means, but where dictatorships use brute power to oppress their own people, and threaten their neighbours the forces of freedom cannot place their trust in declarations alone.

In the course of his article Mr Schultz referred to freedom fighters in Afganistan, Cambodia, Ethiopia, Angola – by a strange co-incidence all of whose struggles could be seen to co-incide with American interests. He did not, however, mention the IRA. This may have been an oversight since what they are fighting for coincides with the noble principles laid down by Mr Schultz – national independence, human rights, freedom from oppression by brute force. Of course it could not be said that they were fighting with American interests in mind.

The Provisional IRA came into being because the politicians both North and South had failed the Nationalist population. They at last realised the terrible truth that the British spurned constitutional means and the only language they understood came from the barrel of a gun. In all the thirty-five countries which Britain forcibly occupied and left, they went only after a bloody war in which literally millions died. Why should the Six Counties be any different? If they leave they will only go as a result of the ballot and the armalite – with emphasis on the armalite. They will not leave as the result of the ballot box only. A long time ago Michael Collins said: 'While England explains the futility of force by others it is the only argument she listens to.' The British have successfully floated the idea that violence does not solve anything, when they know from their long history that it solves far more than constitutional means do. What Britain is really saying is that she and she only can use violence through the SAS, RUC and UDR – but nobody else is permitted to do so. She can brutalise and murder but her victims are only permitted to make constitutional speeches. The IRA may not be all natures's gentlemen but neither are their opponents. Long ago they learned that they 'cannot place their trust in declarations alone' to use Mr Schultz' words. Israel has not been afraid to support the Christian Militia. Why should we not support the IRA in the North? After all they are freedom fighters and did not Margaret Thatcher herself say:

> You have to be prepared to defend the things you believe in and be prepared to *use force* to secure the future of liberty and self-determination (italics mine).

Indeed in 1970 Gerry Boland, who as Minister of Justice had waged a campaign against the IRA, now in the changed circumstances, publicly stated that the government should be training commando-type groups to operate in support of the besieged Nationalist community in the Six Counties. He believed that any self-respecting government with a legitimate territorial claim would do exactly that.

It is not sufficient to be ruthless occasionally with the British. One must hit them again and again between the eyes, relentlessly and constantly. Irish history and indeed world history, proves this over and over again. The principle of Marshall Foch should never be forgotten: 'Attack is the best form of defence'. They do not understand justice or honour – *they only understand force*. In *Operation Brogue* I showed how they walked rings around Irish politicians who gave in to them and gave them everything they asked for while they gave absolutely nothing in return, except torture, blackmail and 3,000 people dead in the Six Counties. They want Northern Ireland for military purposes. They will not be deflected from forcibly occupying it. Despite their polished talk about internal settlements etc. they will not yield one inch. No matter what brutality is required to hold the Six Counties they will not hesitate to use it and where their real brilliance comes is they will get us to support them and in some cases to do it for them.

Every Irish politician should carefully ponder the words of Lloyd George:

> The English are a strong race – they possess the qualities as well as the defects of a strong people. They have a very healthy contempt for the cringing. The man who crawls and creeps about their feet, they spurn and kick, and from the bottom of my heart I admire them for it.

However, it is not just enough to be ruthless with the British. Haughey will need to be ruthless with the Americans too. In recent Anglo-American-Irish relations the Americans have become the messenger boys of the British. When the British fail in a direct approach to the Irish they use the American back-door. In essence approaches made by American politicians are the same as if made by the British. Here again the same ruthlessness will have to be applied. All advances made by American politicians should be suspect – especially offers of financial aid for Northern Ireland.

Finally, Haughey will need to be absolutely ruthless within his own party. This means getting rid of those elements not willing to subscribe to absolute party loyalty. In *Operation Brogue* I wrote:

> Here he will simply have to be ruthless and remember the telling words of the late Marquis of Halifax: 'State business is a cruel trade. Good nature is a bungler in it'. The task now to be attempted is so great that absolute unity and discipline within the party is essential. Nothing short of the type of unity De Valera was able to count on in 1932 will meet the needs of the present day.

Here again I would like to emphasise the importance of bringing men like Niall Blaney back into the party. Blaney knows how to stand up to the British, which is much more than many of the Fianna Fáil front bench do.

Haughey may reckon with certainty that the British will try to destroy him in every way, and with their usual cunning they will try to get Irishmen to do their work for them.

How are they likely to go about it?

Operation Brogue will certainly be re-activated. Since the victory of Haughey in the battle for party leadership MI6 have been licking their wounds and re-grouping their forces for another onslaught, which, with an election coming up in a year or so, is now due.

Another attempt to split Fianna Fáil will almost certainly be made. MI6 believe that there are some in Fianna Fáil more strongly motivated by selfish interests than by Republican ideals and will try to manipulate that element to the fullest. They will not manoeuvre crudely. As is their wont it will be done with subtlety and finesse. 'Britain accepts the right of Fianna Fáil to its Republican principles. That is not in question. What is in question is the unsuitability of Haughey as leader etc.' The line fed will be something like that. What will not, of course, be said is that with Haughey gone the character of Fianna Fáil could revert to what it was in the 1970s, pliable and co-operative and keenly attuned to the British needs. If this happened then the British would be delighted. Fianna Fáil would become a pale green version of Fine Gael, abandoning the half-million Nationalists in the Six Counties and accepting that the role of Irish governments is to be sensitive to the needs of Britain. How far they will succeed in splitting Fianna Fáil is anyone's guess but they will most certainly try and try hard.

When *Operation Brogue* was published I was attacked by many critics for being 'paranoid', 'ludicrous', etc. The very idea that the British would do anything so underhand and debasing as to interfere in the affairs of another nation and try to destroy a leading political figure there was ridiculed and debunked. Let me, therefore, give just one example out of scores where they did just that. I refer to the vilification and destruction of Dr Mussadeq in Iran. For anyone wishing to study this whole saga further I suggest they read *End of Empire* by Brian Lapping, *Something Ventured* by C. M. Woodhouse and an excellent article in the *Irish Times* of 29 May 1985 by Mary Holland, where some details of what happened in Iran are given. In studying these writings readers will be able to judge for themselves whether I or my critics are paranoid.

When Dr Mussadeq decided to nationalise Iran's oil production he dealt a severe blow to the British government who had a substantial greedy interest in controlling that industry. They decided to both vilify and destroy him. This task was entrusted to MI6 who, as usual, gave it a code name, the somewhat ironic 'Operation Boot'.

They began by spreading stories that Mussadeq was an irresponsible lunatic, an unstable megalomaniac, a danger to peace. An orchestrated campaign of grotesque and offensive cartoons followed in newspapers and magazines. They set about making it impossible for Iran to sell oil on world markets and at the same time influencing United States opinion, which had been favourable to Mussadeq, against him by calling him a terrorist.

Enormous sums of money were spent by the British entertaining journalists, editors, politicians etc. in order to win over the media. All this was highly successful and brought about the desired result. The next step was to smuggle in vast sums of money for bribes. The handling of money was put in the hands of three rich Iranian businessmen who succeeded in bribing deputies and senators with *£1.6 million sterling* sent in by MI6. In the end they succeeded in destroying Mussadeq and to crown everything MI6 so manipulated matters that they managed to have Mussadeq arrested and put on trial.

All this is well documented in many publications and one cannot help noticing some similarities with Ireland and with the vilification of Haughey. The great difference is that they defeated Mussadeq while Haughey defeated them. They are not likely to forget this humiliation.

This time the campaign to vilify Haughey is likely to take on a more subtle form. The crude personal attacks that failed so dismally in the past will hardly be repeated. There will, of course, be veiled suggestions that the source of his personal wealth is somewhat suspect. Needless to say not a shred of evidence will be produced to back this up. Indeed if the evidence were properly researched it would probably show that his possessions were acquired by hard work and business acumen. This aspect of his career will be carefully concealed in case the public might jump to the conclusion that his financial and business acumen might be of benefit to the country. Neither, of course, will there be any mention of certain Coalition cabinet ministers whose personal wealth may well be greater than Haughey's nor will there be any deep investigations as to how that wealth was acquired.

More than likely they will encourage attacks on his credibility without even investigating too closely what credibility means – just in case his opponents might not stand up too well to the test.

The wining and dining of journalists likely to write anti-Haughey articles or to slant the news against him may well continue though on a much more modified scale than before. Most journalists now realise that when they are invited to a sumptuous repast the invitation is issued, not because the British think well of them, but because they want to exploit them. The chances are that the British despise them as members of an inferior race but are quite happy to use them to malign and vilify a fellow Irishman. Despite the wariness of most Irish journalists the British will, of course, be able to count on some few who are ever ready to place whatever talents they may have at the disposal of their hereditary enemy in the hope of a few crumbs of praise or an introduction to a titled nincompoop.

They will probably not make any attempt this time to vilify Haughey through Seán Doherty. This seems to have backfired, especially in the fields of phone-tapping and the Dowra affair. It is now known that various Fine Gael dominated governments tapped far more journalists' phones than Seán Doherty ever thought of, and there is very strong evidence to suggest that the whole Dowra affair was a set-up by MI6 to vilify Doherty and thereby help to destroy Haughey. Over the last few years Doherty has emerged as one of the most popular TDs ever in Fianna Fáil and this has been particularly shown by the enormous number of invitations given to him to address various functions, not only in his own constituency, but also in almost every corner in the country. For example, Blarney is a long way from Roscommon but when it was announced that Doherty would attend a function there all tickets were sold out at once, the hall was jammed full with people. MI6 are shrewd enough to realise that vilifying Doherty is now a lost cause.

The old sex angle is unlikely to be revived. There are too many rumours circulating in Dublin concerning the private lives of prominent people in Fine Gael and it may well be that any attack on Fianna Fáil in this field could meet with embarrassing retaliation.

The options open to MI6 this time around are not many unless they can invent or instigate some public trial such as the trial of Mussadeq for treason to try to convince the public that Haughey is untrustworthy and that FitzGerald's sanctity is of the heroic mould even if somewhat lop-sided. This may not be so easy since people in all walks of life are much more aware and wary of the operations of MI6 in Irish political life than they were during the period when Haughey was being vilified.

They may well mount what might be called *Operation Flattery* – that is, a campaign to flatter him, tell him he's the greatest, give him minor concessions dressed up as major ones – much as they did with the Irish delegation in 1921. They will do this in the hope that he may temporarily forget the type of people he is dealing with, and would wish to destroy him by the soft word and choke him with honey and butter. But Haughey has, I believe, learned his lesson, and will not be deceived this time.

It seems to me, and this is purely a personal opinion, that the main line of attack of MI6 at the next election will be that Haughey's Anglo-Irish policy is such that it might well cause a civil war and he is, therefore, untrustworthy. We will not, of course, be told that a civil war here is *exactly what the British want and exactly what the blunders of the Coalition may bring about.* It would be the perfect excuse for them to intervene and in this way acquire the bases on our western seaboard they so urgently need. It is worth looking for a moment at this concept of civil war.

The last civil war in Ireland has not yet been comprehensively documented even though Carleton Younger's excellent book has gone a long way in that direction. There is still a great deal of research to be done on who started it, how the British secret service influenced the murders of the seventy-seven prisoners shot without trial and to what extent that most obnoxious of men and suspected British agent, Tim Healy, ensured that the new government acted with primitive brutality towards all Republican sympathisers, men, women and children.

In a Galway by-election in 1937 Fine Gael accused De Valera of starting the civil war. De Valera answered by suggesting that a special commission of historians and judges be set up to conduct a formal inquiry into the causes of the civil war. Fine Gael refused to participate in such a commission and rejected the suggestion. Why? What had they to hide? What were they afraid might be revealed?

There is considerable evidence that, with the exception of Collins, the new government displayed almost a blood-thirsty obsession with turning the guns on their former comrades. It is now fairly well agreed that General Mulcahy's prohibition on the Convention of Army Officers in 1922 was a major cause in starting the civil war. The track record of Fine Gael in this field is far from edifying.

Future investigations into the origins of the 1922-23 civil war may well show that the founders of Fine Gael and indeed MI6 played a much more decisive role in starting that conflict than has been suspected. In 1934 Ireland once again came close to civil war with the establishment of the Blueshirts, which was a Fine Gael organisation designed to overthrow the democratic institutions of the state.

Very few people know that at that time W. T. Cosgrave, leader of Fine Gael, threatened that under certain circumstances, De Valera and his entire cabinet would be executed. Ireland was only saved then by the wisdom and restraint of De Valera. During the Second World War many of the leaders of Fine Gael, General Mulcahy in particular, made it clear that if Britain invaded Ireland they would not oppose such an invasion. Can anyone doubt the bloody civil war likely to follow such a decision? Unfortunately Fine Gael seem to have a propensity for oppression and indeed, at times, the spilling of blood, as a solution to problems, but only in relation to Republicans. The same medicine is not offered to the Unionists or the British. It was such brutality that goaded the Irish into rebellion in 1798 and surely it would be prudent for us to learn a lesson or two from history. Sadly, however in the field of learning lessons from past events Fine Gael are well at the bottom of the class.

Technical reasons suggest that a distinction be drawn between the Pro-Treaty Party, Cumann na nGaedheal, and Fine Gael, but there is little difference between them. The old Pro-Treaty party had a Republican basis and saw the Treaty as a 'stepping stone' to a Republic. With the mysterious shooting of Michael Collins, Republicanism was abandoned, largely due to the influence of men like Desmond FitzGerald, Earnest Blythe, Kevin O'Higgins and Tim Healy. They settled for a partitioned Ireland, loyalty to the British Crown and a place in the Commonwealth. The Fine Gael party today inherits that philosophy. It has no real commitment to a Thirty-Two county, free, independent Irish nation, and many of its critics see it as the mere ventriloquist's dummy of the British Tory Party. In this sense it is something unique in Europe. I know of no other country which has a large political party whose object is to be subservient to a traditional enemy. This alien attitude is a political minefield and is surely something that could arouse strong opposite passions – passions of the order required to start a civil war.

The ideal of freedom has been an integral part of Irish life for hundreds of years. Again and again the Irish people have been brutalised and crushed to pieces but each time they rose again until finally they got a measure of the freedom they so ardently sought. The operative word here is 'measure'. It is because full freedom is denied them that forces like the IRA are fighting today, and will continue to fight until that freedom is achieved. Whether we like it or not that is the track record of Irish history.

Fine Gael do not seem to be able to learn this simple lesson. By supporting the British in the attempt to hold part of the national territory, and to crush the freedom aspirations of Irishmen North and South, they are perpetrating and encouraging the violence we know today and may well be leading the nation into an extension of that violence to the proportions of a civil war. Fine Gael should remember that it was the Spanish government's obsession with ruling Spain in the interests of Russia which caused the bloodiest civil war of this century. But they are unlikely to do so, and their present muddle-headed attitude may well lead us into the bloodiest of conflicts.

Our ordinary crime rate in Ireland, excluding political offences, is nothing to be proud of. Our cities and towns are rapidly becoming deluged and over-run with drugs. Our old people live in constant terror of being battered to death for a few pounds. Large areas of our cities are ruled by protectionist gangs who demand sums of money weekly from shopkeepers and restaurants under threat of bombing or arson. The stealing of cars and subsequently crashing them, has become a national pastime. One of our great growth areas is the robbing with violence of banks, post offices, shops etc. by armed gangs. In all spheres there is a major breakdown of law and order and no effective action is being taken to deal with these problems. The police have neither the manpower, resources or finances to deal with these criminals, not because these resources are not available – they are – but they are being almost exclusively used, not against criminals, but against Republicans and Nationalists. We spend £1,000,000 a day protecting British interests on the Border, bolstering a criminal regime in the Six Counties, and hounding down Irishmen who escape from that regime. It now seems of more importance to the Coalition to save the life of an SAS or UDR man than it is to save the life of an isolated Irish farmer or an old age pensioner in Dublin.

Some years ago on a trip to London Garret FitzGerald visited a British soldier injured by a bomb in hospital. One cannot but commend this charitable act. Regretfully, however, his charity did not extend to visiting any of the Irish prisoners in British jails, some of whom were at the time being brutalised to a degree reminiscent of Nazi concentration camps.

This unfortunately is hard cold fact. It is not speculation or invention. Our long history proves that brutality towards, and suppression of, our national aspirations was always counter-productive and in most cases led to rebellion.

How far can it be said that we came dangerously close to a civil war during the Forum deliberations? Several 'leaks' suggest that Fine Gael were prepared to go to outlandish lengths to please the British – even to the extent of recognition of the Queen as head of an Irish state, which presumably would mean an Oath of Allegiance. It is said that Haughey ruthlessly axed all these lunacies. If this is correct then the nation owes him a great debt. Had these alleged blunderous proposals of Fine Gael gone through then it is almost certain that Irish blood would once more be spilled by Irishmen on Irish streets. One cannot blind oneself to the possibility of a civil war which becomes dangerously close with each new Coalition blunder. It would also be foolish to ignore the 250,000 unemployed with nothing but a bleak future before them, and the knowledge that protecting British interests is more important than job creation. This is a highly explosive situation which could very easily burst into the flames of a civil war.

As we needed the statesmanship of De Valera in 1934 to prevent a civil war, so we now need the statesmanship of a man like Haughey who understands the national aspirations, whose balance and political vision can defuse a far more dangerous situation than most Irish people realise. Civil war can be avoided by a high national morale, a re-activating of the ideals upon which the nation was founded, and not by brutality, oppression and genuflecting to the British.

The Irish people are weary and tired of being manipulated and exploited by tricky politicians trying to pull off deals and strokes to strengthen their own power bases and copper-fasten their obscene junkets and massive perks and pensions. It is all the more odious when this is done under the guise of rectitude and moral righteousness for this brings the very concept of integrity into disrepute. The people now want the politicians to be reasonably honest – it would be naïve to expect them to be totally honest – the kind of honesty and integrity experienced in the early days of De Valera and Fianna Fáil. I remember those days. As a boy living in a farming community I saw farmers selling their calves for five shillings (twenty-five pence) each, forced to do so by the most terrible British economic war waged to bring the Irish people to their knees; and all the while the then Fine Gael party were helping the British. Yet those farmers, despite their losses, went out and voted for Fianna Fáil. In a letter to Joe McGarrity at the time De Valera said:

> You know that the English are in all this; that they are in touch with the opposition leaders; that a definite plan of campaign is being followed and that disaster awaits the country if the stupidity that is manifesting itself is allowed to continue. On the other hand if we win this fight England will never attempt to squeeze us in this way again.

Today, as in those far off days, to revive our country and shake off the British yoke requires the sure steady hand of a statesman of the highest calibre. Is Charles Haughey that man? He has the ability. He has the political acumen. He does not grovel before the British. Like every outstanding leader in the past he has been maligned and vilified by the media – a sure sign of greatness. All his public pronouncements indicate that he has that love of country required in a great Irish leader. Surely he deserves a chance?

If through the machinations of MI6, or for any other reason he should fail, then the outlook for Ireland could be nightmarish. In 1977 the Irish people trusted Fianna Fáil, gave them a massive victory – and Fianna Fáil failed them. Again in 1982 they put their trust in a Fine Gael Coalition, who again failed them. They are now set to give Charles Haughey a substantial victory in the next election. If for any reason he fails, they may not put their trust again in any of the main political parties. Where or to whom the Irish will turn then is anyone's guess.

It is my hope, and I am sure it is the hope of millions of Irish men and women at home and abroad, that he will succeed. If he does, then Irish history books for the next thousand years will record him as one of the really great Irish statesmen and

Pearse's words, which Haughey himself has so often quoted, will not remain scattered in our polluted air:

> O wise men riddle me this; what if the dream come true.
> What if the dream come true; and if millions unborn shall dwell
> In the house that I shaped in my heart. . .

POSTSCRIPT

As the last pages of this book were being printed the much trumpeted summit between Margaret Thatcher and Garret FitzGerald took place on Friday 15 November 1985. It was a resounding victory for the British and, as I suggested in the Introduction, it would have been better if it never took place. Once more we were out-witted and out-manoeuvred into giving everything and getting nothing — not even our aspirations to unity are given legal status although everything favourable to Britain is. The Irish presence in Belfast, which was hyped as a great gain, is in reality a major disaster. The British will now be able to continue their corrupt system, shoot-to-kill policy, oppression of the minority and at the same time sell world opinion the idea that the Irish government has a say in Northern affairs, a presence in Belfast and that everything is normal. According to well informed sources this idea of a 'presence' was floated by the British and the Irish fell for it hook, line and sinker. It was a major diplomatic triumph for the British.

The aftermath of the summit was intriguing in that nobody except Mr Haughey seems to have spotted the orchestration of praise for the agreement from leaders of various countries. It was almost as if they were all waiting under starter's orders, and when the starter's gun was fired they all rushed with unseemly haste into print. It was somewhat extraordinary that most of these leaders were either pro-British or pro-NATO. Now why would the leaders of NATO countries break precedent with the past and praise this agreement with such faultless timing? Could it be that their interests were other than platonic? Could it be that it brought the Irish people nearer to becoming cannon fodder?

Why would Ronald Reagan give five hundred million dollars in aid on foot of this agreement? Does he love the leprechauns and shamrocks of Ballyporeen all that much or is there another more sinister reason? What a pity some sections of the Irish media did not apply themselves more diligently to these matters, instead of trying to wrong-foot Haughey!

However those who oppose this calamitous agreement should not be too upset. Mr Haughey has promised that he will repudiate it, in its present state, when he gets into power. In doing so he will redeem the honour, integrity and safety of the Irish people.

OPERATION BROGUE
John M. Feehan

This book examines some recent events in the political life of Charles Haughey and questions the role played by the British Secret Service in a campaign of denigration against him. It also examines how far the media gave a one-sided account of events to the detriment of Mr. Haughey and suggests a lot of pertinent questions which they should have asked but did not. Finally it looks at Mr Haughey's role in the future and examines the question as to whether he is the only person capable of leading the country.

THE RISE AND DECLINE OF FIANNA FAIL
Kevin Boland

Fianna Fail was once a proud, idealistic and disciplined party whose first aim was 'to secure the unity and independence of Ireland as a Republic.'

Has there been a complete reversal of the policies on which it was founded — and if so, is disintegration the only future ahead for the party?

FINE GAEL : BRITISH OR IRISH?
Kevin Boland

Do Fine Gael consider themselves enlightened realists against thick-headed diehards, the upholders of law and order against rebels and subversives, of peace against violence? In this book Kevin Boland analyses Fine Gael's philosophy and how it differs from other parties.